I have known and admired Bob Shank for at least a couple of decades. He is one of the master teachers of our time. *LifeMastery* is a wise and accessible condensation of the lessons he has taught thousands of intensely busy and successful people who are seeking to take control of the second half of their lives.

BOB BUFORD
Author, *Halftime* and *Finishing Well*
Founder, Leadership Network

Bob Shank has spent the greater part of his adult life building into others as a teacher, confidant and mentor with one goal in mind: using all the resources God has blessed him with to make an impact for the cause of Christ and His kingdom in their circle of influence. He has done so by making Jesus, the Master Teacher, and His principles the focus of a strategy for a meaningful life that makes a difference both in and through people for today, tomorrow and all eternity.

DENNY BELLESI
Founding Pastor, Coast Hills Community Church
Co-founder, Kingdom Assignment International
Senior Leadership Associate, Slingshot Group

Jesus is proof that each of us has an opportunity to ascend toward God, through Him. He lived out the full potential that God placed in His unique roles as both man and God. We fall far short of that, but we too have God-given DNA that invites us to greater intimacy and an ever more fulfilling life. That journey is the best ride available on the planet and brings us to a final, short step into eternity. For those interested in the journey, Bob Shank is a superb guide and maps out the ascent in this great book.

JAY BENNETT
Vice Chairman, The Bob Buford Institute, Halftime and The Leadership Network, and the National Christian Foundation

God creates each one of us as unique, and part of His design is a calling to leverage who we are to change the world. Bob Shank has written a great book from the life of Jesus to help us identify this unique calling. Bob has been doing this for decades—helping people find their purpose in life, defining what that means and, most importantly, doing something about it. Each page is written with time-tested wisdom. You've got to read this one.

KENTON BESHORE
Senior Pastor, Mariners Church

Bob and I had a chat some years ago when he was in the formative stages of developing the principles found in this book. I had wandered off course a bit, and Bob had the courage to get in my face and say, "Carty, your wood is wet!" He was right. I had lost my fire. His was the stimulus that got me back on track. I know the principles in this book really work. I am living proof.

JAY CARTY
Evangelist and Co-author, *Coach Wooden's Pyramid of Success*

Bob Shank has been a mentor to me for over a decade through The Masters Program. He has brought that teaching to life in *LifeMastery*. We live in a world that pushes us to work longer, stronger, harder and faster. In exposing the model of Christ, Bob exposes His way of peace and purpose. It is not about doing more but about finding our passion and staying on mission. This is a resource that should be on every leader's bookshelf. Get ready to live life on purpose!

DAVE CHEATHAM
Co-founder and Managing Principle, Velocity Retail Group and Accelerated Development Company

In *LifeMastery*, Bob Shank provides an inspired yet practical blueprint to live life enriched with meaning and purpose. Learn how living an intentional life like Jesus did—and clarifying your unique purpose—will set you on a fulfilling life journey.

STEVE FEDYSKI
President and CEO, Pinnacle Forum

LifeMastery will break the chains of anyone who is enslaved by the cruel master of busyness. True freedom comes from examining the mission and purpose of Jesus Christ, the most purpose-driven person in history, and doing a careful assessment of your own abilities, inclinations and resources to discover your unique purpose. From that will flow your vision, mission and goals, leading to intentional, purpose-driven living and true freedom.

BARRY H. COREY
President, Biola University

Bob Shank has spent much of his life studying success and mentoring those in pursuit of it. In *LifeMastery*, he offers clarity to the challenge of creating order and balance in a life often controlled by others' demands. Anyone desiring to live on purpose will be encouraged and enlightened by *LifeMastery*.

MARK DEMOSS
Founder and President, The DeMoss Group
Author, *The Little Red Book of Wisdom*

Bob Shank has been a friend of mine for close to 30 years and serves on the Samaritan's Purse Board of Directors. He has given his life to mentoring people who desire to know God's purpose and develop biblically based goals so their lives can be God-directed. In *LifeMastery*, he sets forth principles and guidelines to challenge readers to consider how they invest their time, effort and talent to live the Christian life with purpose and to influence others for Christ.

FRANKLIN GRAHAM
President and CEO, Samaritan's Purse
  and the Billy Graham Evangelistic Association
Author, *Rebel with a Cause*

Bob Shank has been a mentor to hundreds of people for decades. He is a man whose life I have endeavored to emulate because of his uncompromising commitment, at all levels, to God-honoring excellence. *LifeMastery* is not simply a book that you will read but also a mission you will embrace.

DAVE DIAS
Founder, Insurance Thought Leadership
Vice President, InterWest Insurance Services

Bob Shank does a wonderful job of helping us clearly define our mission in life. Having done that, he shows us how to most effectively manage our daily lives to accomplish that mission.

PAUL ESHLEMAN
Vice-President, Campus Crusade for Christ International

In *LifeMastery*, Bob boils life down to its irreducible minimum and provides the kind of insight that is nothing short of life-altering. Communicating with his typical clarity, his words are soaked in years of real-life experience and a solid understanding of Scripture. No one does well with aimless living, and Bob will show you the difference between merely setting goals and living by a strategic mission. He will have you evaluating yourself in the healthiest way possible—*with hope!*

SKIP HEITZIG
Senior Pastor, Calvary Albuquerque
Author, *Godprint: Making Your Mark for Christ*

Bob Shank is a tremendous communicator, an excellent assessor of life's dizzying array of activity and events, and a great and strategic champion for the kingdom of God! Bob's thoughts and expressions are as provocative, insightful and motivational as anyone I know. *LifeMastery* reveals amazing insights into the life of Jesus—the most unique and intriguing life in history—and shows us how He leveraged everyday situations into eternal stories that exceed time itself. This book is a must-read!

JAN JANURA
Co-founder and Chairman, CAbi Clothing

I like to read books by people who have lived the message. Bob Shank has done so. Even more, I like to read about the most pivotal human in history. Jesus lived a life of purpose and love. This message will help each of us who have been blitzed by a world of consumerism, selfishness and busyness. Enjoy exploring the wiser way—the loving way—of living like the Master.

JEFF KEMP
Vice President and HomeBuilder Catalyst, FamilyLife

For 20 years, I've watched Bob Shank live his life reflecting the principles he writes about in *LifeMastery*. I've served on numerous ministry boards with him, and I've seen the fruits of his work as a mentor to Christian leaders. He has been a true friend to me and given me amazing insights and encouragement from Scripture. Bob is not about advancing his own agenda but about advancing God's kingdom. In *LifeMastery,* he shares those same principles that have helped so many. I know this book will impact your life for time and eternity. I highly recommend it.

GREG LAURIE
Senior Pastor, Harvest Christian Fellowship
Author, *Lost Boy: My Story*

For three years, I was privileged to sit under Bob Shank's tutelage as part of The Masters Program, an executive coaching course for Christian business leaders. He has a unique talent for encouragement and teaching, and he has captured the essence of this teaching in this fast-paced, easy-to-read book. *LifeMastery* is a must-read for anyone who struggles with balancing *success* with *significance*.

PAT MCKINNEY
Managing Partner (Retired), Kiawah Island Real Estate

Having spent more than 10,000 hours coaching people through a Halftime transition from success to significance, I believe this book is a powerful guide to a life of greater meaning, joy and impact.

LLOYD REEB
Author, *From Success to Significance*

LifeMastery is focused and moves from the theoretical to the practical in swift progression. It provides next-step exercises and concrete examples of how current business leaders, famed historical figures, and those who follow the teachings of Jesus Christ can live out those principles and lessons. Bob shows how these three provide the necessary focus and insights for personalizing the exercises to begin living a life of purpose. So go for it and have fun on the journey!

PETER OCHS
Chairman, Fieldstone and First Fruit, Inc.

Meeting Bob Shank and experiencing The Masters Program more than a decade ago proved to be a defining moment in my life. The principles of *LifeMastery*, in addition to the real-time evidence of fruitfulness in Bob's own life, adjusted, refined and focused the trajectory of my own course. For anyone wired by God to lead or for anyone who finds himself or herself in a position of leadership, this book should find its way to the top of your list of must-reads.

STEVE STENSTROM
Former NFL Quarterback and President, Pro Athletes Outreach

Bob Shank has provided a practical perspective on the life and teaching of Christ in *LifeMastery*. God has uniquely gifted Bob with the ability to capture and communicate timeless truths in a manner that makes them accessible and memorable—thereby making us more likely to incorporate them into our daily living. *LifeMastery* is for those who are serious about Kingdom impact!

STEVE STROOPE
Lead Pastor, Lake Pointe Church and Author, *Tribal Church*

Life, as designed by God, was meant to have a transcendent and meaningful direction for us. Yet we often feel as though we are missing the mark, or are constantly starting over. Bob Shank's guidance, experience and wisdom provides a clear path toward a life that truly makes sense. The ideas in *LifeMastery* are biblical, they work, and this book is a major contribution.

JOHN TOWNSEND
Leadership Consultant and Bestselling Author, *Boundaries*

LIFE
MASTERY

**DISCOVER THE TIMELESS
SECRETS FOUND IN HISTORY'S
GREATEST LIFE STORY**

BOB SHANK

FOUNDER, THE MASTER'S PROGRAM

Regal

For more information and
special offers from Regal Books, email us at
subscribe@regalbooks.com

Published by Regal
From Gospel Light
Ventura, California, U.S.A.
www.regalbooks.com
Printed in the U.S.A.

Library of Congress Cataloging-in-Publication Data
Shank, Bob.
  Lifemastery : discover the timeless secrets found in history's greatest life story /
Bob Shank.
      p. cm.
  Includes bibliographical references and index.
  ISBN 978-0-8307-6518-8 (tradepaper : alk. paper)
  1. Christian life. I. Title.
  BV4501.3.S49 2012
  248.4—dc23
  2012031562

Rights for publishing this book outside the U.S.A. or in non-English languages are administered by Gospel Light Worldwide, an international not-for-profit ministry. For additional information, please visit www.glww.org, email info@glww.org, or write to Gospel Light Worldwide, 1957 Eastman Avenue, Ventura, CA 93003, U.S.A.

To order copies of this book and other Regal products in bulk quantities, please contact us at 1-800-446-7735.

To Cheri, my partner in life and purpose.

"Make my joy complete by being like-minded,
having the same love,
being one in spirit and purpose."

PAUL OF TARSUS, PHILIPPIANS 2:2

CONTENTS

ACKNOWLEDGMENTS

For most people, writing a book will forever be a personal mystery. While everyone is living a story, the vast majority will never put theirs down on paper. Some people know an author, but only a few will ever become one. Though writers are an infrequent exception, none of them create a manuscript without the assistance and input of their cultural community.

The essence of *LifeMastery* comes from a book I wrote—with help—in 1990. Originally titled *Total Life Management*, it captured the core message of the ministry I had then—more than 20 years ago—with business and professional leaders. That core message has been refined and sophisticated from that time to the present.

More than 20 centuries ago, the apostle Paul's writings recognized that the best messages are received from someone with wisdom, then passed to others as wisdom: "The things you have heard me say in the presence of many witnesses entrust to reliable men who will also be qualified to teach others" (2 Tim. 2:2). What I wrote about in 1990—and what I've refreshed and written in this book—is the aggregate of understandings passed to me by a succession of reliable men who were qualified to do so.

Beginning with my father-in-law, Jack Kinney, and continuing with the contributions of Loren Griset, Ted De-Moss, Chuck Swindoll, Howard Hendricks, Ross Rhoads and Bob Buford, I can trace the conclusions I present as powerful in this book to those men who mentored me over the last 40 years.

Some of those men have preceded me to heaven; others are still here, continuing to deliver wisdom to reliable men who are qualified to teach others . . . and the process that the apostle Paul described continues on this side of heaven.

In *LifeMastery*, you will be reintroduced to the greatest figure of history, the Lord Jesus Christ. I refer to Him as the ultimate purpose-driven life; I used that term in *Total Life Management* 14 years before my friend Rick Warren made it famous in his book with that title. We are both passing along wisdom that is not original to us, but is sourced in the faith life founded in the model of the Master.

My life continues to be refined by the wisdom invested in me by those whose lives bear evidence of godly insight. It is my prayer this book will be that to you as well.

GOAL OVERLOAD

Bottom line: *You get what you pay for.* Most people in the twenty-first century invest a lot of time and money to maximize their career potential. But, while equipped to pursue a professional horizon, many begin to sense an underinvestment in something even more significant: what they must do to maximize their *life* potential. What if you find yourself winning in business but losing in life?

The man across the hotel restaurant breakfast table was a picture of success. Brad had built his company over the last 15 years into a recognized leader in the high-tech industry he helped to pioneer. He arrived at breakfast that morning in a new European sedan that sported aftermarket wheels and tires worth more than his employees make in a month. Our mutual friend who had arranged this meeting had briefed me enough to let me know that Brad was a locally famous guy with some big-time hurts.

As he lightly buttered his bagel, Brad unfolded for me the story of his professional rise. Born to be a deal maker, his current job description no longer contained the things that made his work fun. The tedium of managing an organization had replaced the thrill of the hunt, and he didn't like it. He shook his head as he told me about a corporate entity that had become a burden instead of a prize.

Things weren't much better on the home front. His marriage was showing signs of wear. A wife who had met the tests of compatibility years before, now little resembled the beach-loving girl he married. Today, two active kids defined her life, and Brad wasn't there nearly enough to pull what she thought was his part of the load. He had given them all the goodies, but they weren't squealing with satisfaction.

"Guys with stress at work and stress at home need a break," Brad told me. He described a group of buddies who shared his frustration with the price of life in the fast lane. Their incomes allowed regular escapes, which had conveniently become men-only by definition. They were tired all-stars in search of a respite, but my new friend told me it wasn't working.

Two things had precipitated Brad's agreeing to meet with me. One was an opportunity to expand his business into its next phase of growth—but it was a move that would put him in airports and hotel rooms, more often than not, for the next five years. Dynamic growth has its price, and Brad was going to have to pay it if he decided to answer this opportunity's knock. Was he willing to ante up? Would his family buy in or blow out?

The other situation was a heart problem known only to him. Not the physical variety, but the romantic kind. A consultant employed by his corporation was helping him update a business plan for the expansion, and their professional relationship was beginning to assume a different tone. Brad was feeling the tug of the hormones.

The consultant, a competent MBA from a major West Coast university, was the best he had ever met in her field. Young, confident and in tune with the contemporary corporate culture, she had plugged into his mind on a frequency his wife had never been able to attain. Though nothing had happened yet, he knew that it was only a matter of time before one thing led to another. A distant backdrop to this nightmare was a sense of moral responsibility that nagged at him relentlessly. As a college student, Brad told me, someone had confronted him with the historic Christian faith. After weeks of exploring his "What about?" questions, and enjoying the company of a campus fellowship of Christians, he had decided to join them in their relationship with God.

He still acknowledged his faith—albeit nominally—through a socially acceptable church in the community. But his convictions hadn't offered any earthshaking solutions to his confusion. They had only served to unsettle him as he watched the options exercised by his peers. A number of his friends had abandoned any beliefs or constraints that inhibited their freedom for a self-serving, midlife revolution. "I know that some of the things I'm considering aren't the best," he told me "but I find myself entertaining them anyway."

Life for Brad wasn't fun anymore. The price required for success was no longer a good deal. His friends who had made radical moves in response to the same hopeless emotions were bigger basket cases afterward than they were before. Brad was sincere: He wanted to know what to do.

What do you say to a guy who has achieved all of his goals and now wants to know why it feels so empty?

The Great American Nightmare

This wasn't the first time I'd heard such a combination of woes from a person whose life seemed to be the picture of success. America seems to be growing a bumper crop of men and women who find themselves winning in business and losing in life. Trained as technicians, prepared to spin the dials and work the system, they've got the machine spitting out big checks with their names on them, but the thrill is long gone.

America seems to be growing a bumper crop of men and women who find themselves winning in business and losing in life.

There are a lot of people today who do very well between 8:00 AM and 5:00 PM. You may see their pictures in the business section of the local newspaper—or *The Wall Street Journal*—announcing their most recent promotion. They have probably been featured in some industry-wide publications that heralds them as the up-and-comers in their specialties. They are the folks asked to lead the workshops and seminars when their industry convenes.

Then there comes the traumatic moment when they have to leave the office and reenter real life. The prominence they enjoy in the marketplace is about to be replaced by an intense sense of dysfunction. Their workplace contemporaries tell them they are successful, but privately they admit their capability ends at the business door.

It is possible to win at business but lose at life. It happens every day to people you know. It may even be happening to you.

It certainly was happening to Brad. Just imagine: a guy with a business degree, a great company, a six-figure income, a cute wife, healthy kids, a gymnast's physique . . . yet miserable. *Only in twenty-first century America!* He wouldn't evoke much sympathy from most people who view him as a model for their own lives instead of a victim of the system.

It was my turn to talk. With my breakfast growing cold, the conversation began to warm up. I told Brad I understood how he felt. For me, it had happened years before, but I could still remember asking the same kinds of questions and feeling similar emotions. I colored for him a picture of my public accomplishments and private concerns.

By the time I had been out of school for a decade, I had blitzed some of the big decisions of life and gotten lucky, or so it seemed. The company I joined in 1970 had become the focus of my career. This privately held corporation dominated its field in our part of the state. I had taken over the operation from the owner to allow for his semiretirement. My title was "executive vice president," but I ran the firm like it was my own. Business had grown 400 percent in the five years I had been responsible. I had assembled a great management team, and they were humming.

With nearly 300 employees, innumerable clients and attentive vendors, I never lacked for someone who wanted a piece of my time. The protocol of leadership carried certain personal responsibilities. Relationships founded on the working environment ate up mealtimes and social opportunities.

Visibility in the industry also meant giving something back. Though volunteer service on standards committees and professional associations was sometimes a nuisance, it was junk food for the ego. I was developing an impressive multi-page résumé.

Cheri and I had been married for nearly a decade by then. Our two daughters, both under age seven, kept her occupied while I pursued my own agenda away from home. A succession of high-demand hobbies occupied all the discretionary time I could spare. Distance running, with quarterly marathon competitions, and private white-water rafting adventures on western rivers consumed my attention during hours away from work.

I related to Brad's spiritual heritage as well. A Christian since my youth, I found satisfaction participating in a variety of ways with our local church, as well as through some Christian business organizations. In fact, some of my deepest fulfillment came from the people I knew in these capacities. It felt good when dormant feelings of selfless service began to surface.

You don't do all of that without managing your time well. My wife and I were masters at cramming activity into compact schedules. Friends were in awe of our itinerary. "I don't know how the two of you do it," won the prize for the most-expressed comment by guests around our dinner table.

Back then, if you had looked up *goal-oriented* in an encyclopedia, I think you would have found our pictures in the margin. We were setting goals and clicking them off. If you could mount goals on the wall as you fulfilled them, our family room would have been lined with trophies. Boy, could we pursue goals.

As for my wife, the stories of her room-mother roles, her service as field-trip concierge at the kids' private school and her leadership of a women's organization were constantly replenished. The recitation of her meritorious deeds were matched by my tales of business deals and weekend expeditions "where no man has gone before."

But we were disaster in the making. The words, "ships passing in the night" sounded like a colorful exaggeration when she would say it, but Cheri was right. We were greeting each other's vapor trails as we came and went every day. Something had to give.

A Time for Reappraisal

That nagging sense of deficiency finally gave birth to a summit conference. It was the fall of the year, and Cheri and I had hit the end of our rope. I booked a weekend for us at a desert resort, then called home and announced the challenge: "We're going away for the weekend to make some sense out of this life we've got out of control. And we're not coming back until we have an answer!"

At this juncture, my breakfast buddy, Brad, was leaning forward into the story. I could see him spotting the similarities in our lives. The *"nobody's been through this and lived!"* look was fading from his face. "What happened?" he interrupted. "What did you do when you got to Palm Desert?"

I told him what Cheri and I did that weekend and how it literally changed our lives. Our crisis made us analyze the problem and forced us to find some permanent solutions. In time, we began telling others what we'd learned. We've watched this principle bring order and direction to people who had most everything they thought they wanted from life . . . except *contentment*.

The more we were able to help others, the more my business career began to fade in importance. Eventually, I left my "perfect" job to work full-time helping people achieve significance after they recognize there is more to life than just "success."

Significance and balanced life management are not elusive dreams. Over a period of several weeks, I was able to guide Brad through a few basic exercises that produced a new game plan for his life. This time it was balanced. Some of the changes were hard to implement emotionally, but Brad persevered. A renewed love for his life, his family and his business were the benefits that motivated him to make these changes permanent.

You, too, can bring order and balance to your frantic existence. The spark *can* be renewed in a fading marriage. There is a reason for life that goes beyond the next big deal. You *can* discover how to sort through the confusing and conflicting demands of people and projects. If you feel locked inside a maze, *there is an escape.*

> If you feel locked inside a maze,
> *there is an escape!*

I invite you to invest just a few hours exploring the principles in this book. If you do, I promise you will discover a fresh outlook on life. And if you take some time to do the suggested LifeMastery exercises, you will find yourself regaining control of your future.

LifeMastery is not a dream. It's a real possibility. It begins by addressing a fundamental prerequisite. Fulfill this and you'll unlock a secret most people never discover—a secret that opens the doors to LifeMastery.

] 2 [

THE MISSING
PREREQUISITE

A silver-haired man walks onto the stadium field and stops beside the groundskeeper who is raking the cinders on the third-base path. "Looks like the doubleheader won't be a sellout," he says to the workman.

"Best seats in the place are still in the dugout," comes the reply.

The distinguished looking stranger walks on, heading to the dugout under the empty stands, his steps making a visible path through the morning dew on the infield grass. He reaches into the bat rack, pulls out a manila envelope and sits down on the bench. Inside the envelope is a small tape player containing a cued reel of audiotape. After he turns on the machine, he opens a smaller envelope that was packed along with the tape recorder. Out of it fall several black-and-white glossies.

"Good morning, Mr. Phelps. The man with the turban is the Omar of Lasagna. A radical group headed by Abra Cadabra, shown here with his two wives, has threatened the Omar of Lasagna's leadership. If Cadabra and his front for the Liberation of Lasagna are successful, it will mean the destabilization of the entire region. Your mission, Jim, if you choose to accept it, is to neutralize the opposition to the Omar's administration and assure the peace of Lasagna. As always, Jim, if you or any member of your IMF are apprehended, the secretary will disavow any knowledge of your actions. Good luck, Jim." A hiss and then a plume of smoke follows the recorded message as the tape self-destructs.

The *Mission: Impossible* movie trilogy has its roots in a television series. From 1966 to 1973, weekly viewers watched Peter Graves accept his Mission: Impossible assignment, confident of his willingness to tackle the most incredible challenges. The television screen never went blank during prime time; he never declined a mission. And there was never any question about what the outcome would be. It was fascinating to discover the details of his strategy for success, but you could always count on the results. The mission was always accomplished.

Week in and week out, the IMF agents had a mission statement that directed their activities. This fictional team knew what options fit the mission and which ones didn't, based on their contribution to the fulfillment of the mission. The members' ability to order their lives while engaged in the mission was consistent and deliberate.

Could it be that our lives often end in tragedy because we lack the same kind of focus?

This book is a book with a mission. Here is my three-fold purpose:

1. To help you see the immense importance of defining a mission statement for your life;

2. To help you formulate a personal life mission statement;

3. To show you how to go about managing your life in keeping with your mission.

Goals Aren't Enough

Let me tell you from the onset that this is not another book about setting goals. I have read books, attended seminars and invested weeks of my adult life in service to goals. Sadly, most of that time has produced more frustration than fruit. Let me explain.

One seminar directed me to break my life into bite-sized nuggets; every dimension that demanded time and energy deserved a separate goal. I made the typical list:

- Professional
- Marital
- Familial
- Financial
- Spiritual

- Physical
- Educational
- Charitable
- Recreational

Your list may vary some, but everyone's list is similar. I learned how to explore each of these areas in order to construct clear, measurable goals for each one. My life, I was told, was going to be enhanced by my ability to see personal progress in each of these important facets of my life.

If you had dropped in on me during those years, you would have found my goals clearly defined. I knew where I was going in each of these dissimilar areas. I was on my way.

Managing my time became a function of advancing my goals. That's when some of my problems set in. It seemed that some of my goals weren't getting along with one another. That's putting it mildly; the truth was, some of them were fighting like cats and dogs.

Goals at War

Let me illustrate this struggle with three things that I was pursuing:

1. *Professionally,* we were trying to increase our profits in the midst of a shrinking market. That meant I needed to spend more time at the office, shaving expenses and increasing margins through better quality contracts with clients who needed to see me personally. If I wanted to realize my professional goals, I needed to commit myself.

2. *Physically,* I was trying to reduce my marathon times. My training schedule had me running about 50 miles a week. That amount needed to go up to 70 if I was going to achieve my objective; I needed to find another four hours a week to devote to training.

3. *Personally,* I was committed to spending more time with my daughters, who were increasingly aware of my absence and knew enough to ask

where I was. If they were going to be impressed with their dad and view me the way I wanted to be viewed, they needed more time with me. I couldn't delegate this project to anyone else— these were my children.

There you have it, three *bona fide* arenas of life with three simple and understandable goals. No glaring problems with these, right? *Wrong!*

Goals don't just happen, they require strategies: Stay at the office just one more hour each day; arrive home at 6:00 instead of 5:00; sprint up the stairs, suit up in my Nikes and wind suit for the last rays of daylight, and hit the streets. Stretch my daily hour training run by a half hour to get the mileage base up. Sail back home, dripping sweat and in need of a cool-down period, to see the family sitting around the dining room table, waiting for dinner to convene 90 minutes later than it used to. Wolf down my chow, try to stimulate meaningful small talk with the tiring troops and then pack the munchkins off to bed by their 8:30 PM bedtime.

....

Have you ever debated the merits
of your plans for career enrichment or
your invigorated exercise program
when faced with a life partner
who wants to know where she and
your progeny fit in?

....

Oh, the joys of the goal-oriented life! Have you ever debated the merits of your plans for career enrichment or your invigorated exercise program when faced with a life partner who wants to know where she and your progeny fit in?

And that was only three of the areas! There was more to it for me, as there is for you. The more complex your life mix, the more bizarre the potential problems. I had defined numerous areas of my life that qualified for designated, defined goals. Talk about tension: I couldn't pursue a single one of the goals without feeling competition from other goals.

Don't think for a minute that those difficulties are reserved for the married members of our go-for-it-all generation. There are lots of never-married, childless men and women whose life demands are just as daunting as mine were. Or, if you're a single adult whose children split time between each parent's household, the wheels are even more likely to come off the get-it-all-done life demands that confront them daily.

So, where are you feeling the tension?

- You may feel it in your compulsion to "pay your dues" at the office by working far into the night until you get the promotion.

- You may notice it most when you fall asleep over textbooks for the classes you've got to finish this semester to get your degree in June.

- You may experience it when you're waiting for a six-year-old to spit out a story over breakfast while you're waiting to leave for an important meeting.

- You may discover it lurking alongside you as you sleep in with your spouse on Sunday while feeling guilty about not being at church where your mom always said you belonged.

My goals, originally intended to increase my satisfaction with life, were traumatizing me. Each of them called for my attention, making a rational case for priority in my schedule.

Achievement even began to betray me. Goals accomplished simply put me on new ground from which to view the next higher range. Closure gave way to expanded demands. My goals had become gremlins that were fighting with one another and gnawing on my mind. Obviously, my goals needed to be synthesized, but that hadn't been part of the training!

Which goals really fit in my life? How could I pursue these positive promises of a bright future and select the right combinations that would get along with one another?

I discovered the answer in the formulation of a "life purpose" statement.

The Foundation for Goals

During our summit conference in the desert, Cheri and I spent the bulk of two days exploring the answers to three questions:

1. What unique gifts, resources and talents did we bring to our marriage? What were the things we could do better than anything else?

2. What had we learned about our natural personal tendencies? How did we work best with one another and with other people? In what environments were we most effective?

3. For what did we have a heart? If we could change any single thing in the world through investing our lives in the cause, what would it be?

As best we knew how, we tried to give substance to these intangibles. Our time spent discussing and debating these points allowed us to arrive at a consensus by the time we were finished.

We looked like superpowers trying to agree on a disarmament proposal, but we finally gave birth to a statement we both could own. No one snapped any pictures or played a blast of bugles, but it was in that hotel room that we first crafted a document that we have since come to value as a personal treasure.

It is important to understand exactly what we were doing. We were laying a foundation that would allow us to set realistic goals. The goals came later in the process; they were not the guiding force.

....

We were laying a foundation that would
allow us to set realistic goals.
The goals came later in the process;
they were not the guiding force.

....

The problem was that I had always started with goals rather than ending with them. I had been taught to ask, "What are your goals?" rather than, "What is your purpose?" Here are the elements we found we needed to solve what wasn't working and change our life together for good:

- A **purpose** statement that takes into account how we're qualified, where we're effective and where our passion directs us for the whole of our lives . . . all of what we are, for as long as we are. This gives us a reason for the things we do and the lives we live.

- A **vision** of our future to project our direction as we pursue our purpose. This meets our need to see past today to how we are progressing.

- A sense of **mission** that motivates even the mundane aspects of life, allowing us to see how all things fit into the bigger picture. Mission is purpose in action.

- A clear **strategy** to sharpen our thinking as we constantly assess the resources at hand and the opportunities available to us. This allows us to manage how we invest ourselves in keeping with our life plan.

- Finally, based on those primary foundational conclusions: a reasonable set of **goals** that harmonize rather than clash with one another. These goals make it possible to choose the best areas in which to invest ourselves and to bypass anything less.

Living on Purpose

When's the last time someone looked you square in the eye and asked you to articulate your purpose statement? If you were asked to do that today, how would you answer?

Goals and purpose are apples and oranges. By my independent survey, more than 80 percent of the people willing to answer the question, "What is your life purpose?" gave me a goal rather than a purpose.

One man answered, "My purpose is to retire and travel." That is not a purpose; that is a goal.

Another man said, "My purpose is to be a good husband and father." Great goal, but it's not a purpose.

A woman I interviewed said: "My purpose is to be the first woman on the board of [a prominent organization]." She did it; it was a goal.

So what's the difference between a goal and a purpose?

- A **goal** is always measurable; it can be accomplished within a given period of time and will be replaced by a new goal once achieved. You can have multiple goals at any given time.

- A **purpose** is not measurable, and it is never fully attainable in this life. It will only be refined and restated (never replaced) in your lifetime—if it is the right purpose for you. You will only have one purpose active in your life.

Did you realize that the quality and extent of your life depend, to some degree, on your ability to define your purpose and mission in life?

How would you answer the question "What is your life purpose?" Is there a manila envelope waiting somewhere for you? What would be on the recording when you hear, "Your mission, should you choose to accept it, is _____ _____"?

If you know the answer to that question, you're already ahead of most people. However, don't be discouraged if you can't answer it. I'm going to provide you with a step-by-step plan to help you arrive at your own life purpose statement.

] 3 [

THE VALUE OF
PURPOSE

He inherited his position from his father, who recognized potential in him through early successes. The son was encouraged to use his exceptional abilities to blow out the boundaries and take the operation far beyond the confines that existed when he took over.

At age 20, he became CEO. Within a few years, his vision and innovation directed the troops to new victories and expansive growth. By the time he reached 30, he controlled the market. He was a goal-oriented leader of the first degree. His name was on everything. He was the model of success. He was so successful that he lacked any more worlds to conquer.

Major error: Call your goals your reason for living and then achieve them all. Result: Lose your reason for living.

When that happened to Alexander the Great, history records that he sat down, placed his head in his hands and wept. He met all of his objectives and had nowhere else to go. Soon he grew despondent. His drinking went out of control and he stopped achieving. Three years later, at age 33, he was dead.

Abraham Maslow is remembered for his insights into human psychology. One of Maslow's most fascinating pursuits was his research on the effects of purpose in people's lives. He concluded that both the quality and quantity of life were affected by a person's intensity of purpose. In fact, the length of one's life is directly linked to his or her sense of purpose felt at midlife. In Maslow's observations, if you didn't possess a reason big enough to define your life, you wouldn't live as long as someone who did.

Inadequate Substitutes

In contemporary American society, most people derive their purpose from their activities, rather than deriving their activities from their purpose. *You are because of what you do,* they think. That's backward!

Career-driven men and women who don't consciously decide otherwise nearly always attempt to find their purpose in their work. As long as things are going well in their professional lives, they can weather any storm. Life may be in the bucket, but if their last performance review was positive, they would generally gauge their lives as successful. Withdraw their title or their business card, and you'll shake their foundations. Impugn their proficiency, and they'll begin to wonder about the value of life. These are the people who jump from windows when their bar charts go south.

....

In contemporary American society, most people derive their purpose from their activities, rather than deriving their activities from their purpose. *You are because of what you do,* they think. That's backward!

....

Watch the curious dance of these people when they get their gold watch at retirement. Often, when the dust settles and they have removed their effects from their desk, life is over. They aimlessly wander from hobby to hobby, struggling to find meaning in life. Otherwise healthy men and women die off in droves just a few years after retirement. Why should that surprise us? They simply don't have a big enough reason to live.

Women who elect to emphasize their children rather than a career are not insulated from this syndrome. Defining their lives by their growing kids, they feel great highs and dramatic lows based on the current status of their offspring. When the kids receive their diplomas and head into adulthood, Mom's success as a parent would seem to be assured. Instead, this often triggers a sense of worthlessness and futility in a home-oriented mom; her reason for existence is now obsolete. If the goal of being a good mom to dependent children was her purpose, she is up for grabs emotionally when they become independent. Empty nests often lead to strained marriages, midlife affairs, a return to the workplace in search of meaning, and divorce by the forties.

One of the offbeat curiosities in Los Angeles the Watts Towers. Built in a neighborhood whose glory has long since passed, they are the life work of a man who couldn't part with a good piece of garbage. Hubcaps, Hula-Hoops, toasters and tire irons have found their way into this hodgepodge of Americana. If you look closely, you may find a long-discarded piece of your own history. The Watts Towers are simply the result of disparate pieces strained into synthesis. The outcome is unique as a piece of art, but worthless as a functioning structure.

Any building of value begins with thoughtful design. The architect produces a set of drawings and specifications for the building based on the intent of the structure and the distinctives of the site. Construction elements are chosen in keeping with the plans so that everything comes together to form a truly unique expression of form and function.

Should a life be any less thoughtfully constructed?

A Blueprint for Life

A purpose statement is to life what the architect's model is to the edifice. It gives the rendering, in advance, of the final product as expressed by the designer. A blueprint follows, in which every goal and activity is chosen in keeping with how it will contribute to the overall scheme.

Imagine calling subcontractors and workmen to converge on a construction site with no architectural plans! The finest carpentry job will be meaningless if it is not integrated with every other element of the process. Excellence in the details will be devoid of importance if the finished composite is valueless.

Great buildings are not so designated because of the quality of their parts, but by how those quality pieces fit together in harmony and precision. Great plans are more important than great pieces. In fact, average elements can combine to become magnificent cathedrals!

....

Excellence in the details will
be devoid of importance if the finished
composite is valueless.

....

Here's an interesting exercise: Get a pencil and jot down six of the greatest names in history (*Let me prime your pump: Thomas Edison, Clara Barton, Shakespeare, Joan of Arc, Lincoln, Luther, Galileo, King David. Get the picture?*)

Got a list? Let me ask you a question or two about your names. What one thing distinguishes them for the list? What do you know of their incomes? How about their material possessions? Can you tell me their hobbies or recreational preferences?

Chances are, all of the names of the people on your list are known for a singular cause or contribution they made to civilization and history. I doubt there were any "generalists" on your list—any people who did a lot of things in an above-average way but did nothing exceptionally well. I suspect that most of them were single-minded, driven and sold-out to a particular end for which they gave their all. With regard to their holdings and financial accomplishments, chances are you would have to bury yourself in a library to get a fuzzy answer. Consider the following statement:

The great men and women of history were not great because of what they owned or earned, but rather for what they gave their lives to accomplish.

There's one name that belongs on your list if He isn't there already. Some say He was the most incredible figure of all time. That's really amazing, because He lived and died without writing a book, leading an army, fathering a family or starting a company. He never even traveled beyond the borders of His small country. His name is Jesus of Nazareth.

No life ever demonstrated commitment to purpose more powerfully than Jesus Christ's. No life ever demonstrated the compound impact of purpose more than His. No person ever demonstrated the tranquility and peace that attends the purpose-driven approach more than Jesus. The records of His life, written by four men from four different perspectives, display His exquisite expression of purpose and mission in a way that makes perfect sense.

You might think this to be a book written only for people who already identify themselves as "Christian," whatever that term may mean to you. Let me assure you: If that is your status, this fresh exposé of the distinctives seen through the high-impact years of the earthly life of Jesus will be the basis for some extraordinary discoveries.

Or, you may be Christian friendly, but not yet a card-carrying follower of Jesus. I'm not the first to probe the effective approaches employed by historic leaders with an intent to translate their strategies into contemporary expression. From the late Steve Jobs, twenty-first century technology visionary, to ancient Chinese military strategist and philosopher Sun Tzu, the lessons derived from prior players whose names are now enshrined in culture line the shelves in the business sections of modern bookstores.

Wherever you place yourself on the faith spectrum, there is no denying the fact that this itinerant carpenter from a backwater village miles from nowhere did more to change the world in three years—without a passport or Internet access—than anyone who came before or after Him.

Are you curious enough to ask how a young man without resources or résumé accomplished so much?

Let me introduce you to the most purpose-driven figure of history.

THE LIFEMASTERY MODEL

If there had been a *Jerusalem Post* two thousand years ago, the Jewish people might well have read stories with headlines like these:

Man Turns Wedding into Wine-tasting Party

Mob of 5,000 Pig Out on Boy's Lunch

Walk for Life Reported on Sea of Galilee

Taps Turns to Rap When Boy Crashes His
   Own Funeral

Blind Beggar Passes Eye Test

Back from the Dead: Moses and Elijah Spotted on
Mountaintop

Tiny Taxman Finds Religion in a Tree

If we didn't know better, we'd almost think this was the
National Enquirer or perhaps the *Huffington Post.*

These weren't isolated incidents. Day after day, crowds
were left breathless over the exploits of the man who
claimed to be God.

In some ways, He is an unfair example. If the statements attributed to Jesus and His followers are true, He is
not like you and me. Jesus wasn't just an ordinary guy; He
was the eternal God, born into the race through a young
virgin supernaturally impregnated by God. He was a never-
to-be-repeated phenomenon: the Son of God.

He also planned, however, to be an example. He is presented as the model of what God intended our lives to be.
Jesus constantly enjoined people to follow Him. His followers encouraged people to follow them as they followed
Him. They described Him as a standard of the first order by
which to measure and mold their own lives.

In His deity, He is not duplicable. But in His humanity,
Jesus intends to be duplicated! His followers had various titles they used to describe His role in their relationship;
"Master" was one of them, and they used it often. They lived
to replicate His example.

He did not intend to set a record so astounding we would
not seek to equal it. He intended to leave behind a movement committed to approaching His perfect performance.

Now, I'll be honest with you. I *know* I'll never equal His
mark. But that doesn't prevent me from trying.

In 1978, I ran my first marathon. Intending to run just
the first half as a training exercise. My buddy John and I

felt so good at the midpoint that we went all the way. As we crossed the line together after 3 hours and 31 minutes, we were ecstatic and exhausted.

The next day as I was dressing for work, I wanted to wear the flimsy T-shirt they gave me for finishing the race. Unfortunately, I couldn't figure out how to get my tie on over it. It seemed like my unsophisticated co-workers had never met a marathon runner. These were the two most-asked questions that day:

"You ran a marathon, huh? How long was it?" *What a dumb question! All marathons are the same length—26 miles, 385 yards.*

"Did you win?" *How do you tell someone that the winner crossed the line an hour and 20 minutes before you did, and you feel great about it?*

In 23 marathon finishes since then, I haven't crept any closer to the winner's circle, but that hasn't hindered my competitive spirit. I don't expect to win. But I do expect to do better—at least within my age category! The winner's performance motivates me, even though I know I will never equal it.

Jesus is the winner who ran the perfect, never-to-be-repeated race. He wears the victor's crown today as He watches me run the course and try for a personal best. His approach to the race is the model for my own. I don't expect to better His time; I just want to better *my* time. No human being can exceed Jesus' accomplishments, but He, as the champion, presents His regimen as a model to increase our capacity.

Have you ever looked at the life of Jesus in that way? Have you delved into the human side of God to find the practical insights He put on record for you and me to maximize our lives? That is what I want to do in the rest of this book: examine the perfect model for life on earth and learn from it.

I realize that discussing Jesus and His relevance produces different emotions for different people. For some, the result is reverence; for others, it's ridicule. Perhaps the majority of our world finds itself between those two poles—willing to consider His historic contribution to civilization and culture, but not yet able to relate to Him as God in human flesh.

Let me say it again: Wherever you find yourself on this continuum, I hope you'll read on. If the most you can accept is that the man Jesus started a movement that went global and has survived nearly 20 centuries, there is still much that you can glean from this book. If you regard Him as a personal friend and your eternal Savior, you have even more to gain. So don't let His presence scare you. You can learn something from the life of Jesus, no matter where you are.

> Don't let Jesus' presence scare you. You can learn something from the life of Jesus, no matter where you are.

At the very foundation of the abundant life—part of the promise extended by Jesus to those who find relationship with Him—is this issue of purpose. Jesus knew His purpose on earth. He never made a decision without knowing exactly why He was here and how His actions would affect His mission. Every fragment of His life was in perfect harmony with His purpose. His biographies portray Him as occasionally weary, but never frustrated. He never wasted a minute, never pursued a rabbit trail, never went down a blind alley. He was deliberately resolute.

How long must one live to make an impact? Jesus spent 30 years in obscure preparation for His life's work, and then He had only 3 years to exercise His primary emphasis. Could a man really make a difference in such a short time? Jesus felt He could. On the night before His death, He told His father: "I have brought you glory on earth by completing the work you gave me to do" (John 17:4).

A life mission statement that becomes the working blueprint for constructing a life worth remembering—that's what Jesus had. Let's look at what the biblical accounts tell us about His mission.

His Mission Was Determined Before His Birth

Mary was pregnant but she wasn't married. That's a dilemma in any society. Joseph, her fiancé, wondered what to do, for he knew he wasn't the child's father. In his day, engagement was as binding as marriage and could only be broken through divorce. Being a decent man, Joseph didn't want to expose Mary to public disgrace, so he decided to divorce her quietly.

About this time, an angel appeared to Joseph in a dream. Joseph was told to not be afraid to take Mary as his wife, that the Holy Spirit had conceived her child. He was instructed to name the child Jesus, "because he will save his people from their sins" (Matt. 1:21).

Thirty years passed after the birth of Jesus, and very little is known about those years. In Jewish culture, a man's entry into significance occurred at the age of 30. Before that, you didn't qualify for important leadership in the community. Jesus was God, yet He fit within the confines of His society. He lived a normal life—so normal that, when He returned to His hometown after beginning His public work, they couldn't believe His miracles. For 30 years He hadn't demonstrated anything supernatural. He was biding His time, preparing for the occasion when His mission would be fulfilled.

It's easy to get fired up about some things in life. It's also fun to be creative and to see yourself as an innovator. We can even dream about founding a new movement or ideology. But where does the impetus come from? Whose idea is it, anyway?

Let me suggest a thought. Jesus stepped into a mission that had been formulated before He arrived on the scene. It existed when He was born. As He began His public ministry, His mission awaited Him. Is the same true of you?

The trick is not to *create* a purpose but to *discover* your purpose. Before you were capable of grappling with the concept, the eternal God had a purpose in mind for you within His over-arching purpose for His world. Like Jesus, your task is not to create a purpose but to embrace the one He already has for you!

His Career Began with a Restatement of His Mission

Jesus had a cousin named John, a man we know as John the Baptist. John's job was to prepare society for the arrival of the Messiah. He introduced Jesus as that Messiah: "Look, the Lamb of God, who takes away the sin of the world!" (John 1:29).

Did you enter into your career with clarity about your mission? Did you see how your work fit into your overall direction in life? Or, do you find yourself years into a professional pursuit, never having discovered why you do what you do?

I've been exploring this question for nearly 30 years, and it no longer surprises me to get behind the defensive firewall of many successful careerists only to find that their accomplishments have failed to supply the longing for meaning that haunts them at the core.

If career success could satisfy the soul, ours would be the most fulfilled generation—and the most peaceful society— ever recorded. Instead, our advancement has been accompanied by relational disruptions, chemical addictions and personal destruction. No one blinks when famous people are headlined with words like "divorce," "burnout," "addiction" or "suicide." In an age with so much . . . what's missing?

Jesus began His career with a restatement of what He was about. Several interesting elements add spice to this story. John the Baptist is a key person for many reasons:

- He was a mission-driven person himself. His father had received insight from God about John's specific purpose in life: "You will go on before the Lord to prepare the way for him, to give his people the knowledge of salvation through the forgiveness of their sins" (Luke 1:76-77). John accepted this call to be an advance man for the main event, and he was fulfilled within that mission.

- He was entrusted, through divine revelation, with information about Jesus: the knowledge of who Jesus was and what He was sent to do. Listen to what John said: "I would not have known him, except the one who sent me to baptize with water told me, 'The man on whom you see the Spirit come down and remain is he who will baptize with the Holy Spirit.' I have seen and I testify that this is the Son of God" (John 1:33-34).

- He understood the mission of Jesus. He wasn't telling Jesus something He didn't already know. John's statement was not for Christ's benefit, but for the people standing by, and for us today. Jesus didn't "grow into" the shoes of the Messiah; they were custom-crafted just for Him. He didn't decide to become the Son of God on a mission, He was already designated as the Son of God on a mission.

John represents an independent confirmation of Jesus' mission, in much the same way that the Bible today serves to confirm the mission entrusted to people who claim kinship with the Son of God. Your mission is as foundational to your adult life as Jesus' was to Him!

His Mission Defined Who He Was

Many men and women can only identify themselves in terms of their profession: "I'm a lawyer," "I'm president of ABC Corporation," "I sell cars," "I'm an accountant for Abaloney and Zoe." Is your life defined by the details on your business card?

One of the greatest tragedies is to see the identities of men and women stripped away. One moment they're linked with a prestigious company. Then, one Friday afternoon, they're called into an office and told, "We've decided to make some changes." Suddenly they're cleaning out their desks and feeling like nonpersons. After being escorted to the parking lot, they drive home wondering how to announce the news, and they head straight to their computer to get in the cyberspace line for their next fragile identity.

When your essence is derived from your job or a position in a firm or your salary, your life is shattered when that connection vanishes. Jesus determined His identity based on His mission. It wasn't based on being a carpenter for nearly 20 years. His mission defined who He was.

....

When your essence is derived from your job or a position in a firm or your salary, your life is shattered when that connection vanishes.

....

Think about the way you might have handled the kind of treatment that was typical for Jesus. Had He depended on finding Himself through the acceptance of others, He would have changed His mission. Had He looked for significance through the gratitude of the people He healed and helped, He never would have found security. If human affirmation had been necessary for Him to keep His spirits high, He should have found a different job.

But Jesus found Himself in His mission. His willingness to suffer abuse and rejection were based on His understanding of the cost of that mission. Because His identity was found within His pursuit of purpose, He suffered no internal conflict in His circumstances. His security was as well founded as His commitment to His cause.

His Mission Was Not Easily Understood or Quickly Embraced

For two years, Jesus made His way around the regions of Judea and Galilee. The masses flocked to Him. One big swath of humanity followed His every move.

During this time, He found 12 followers in whom He invested His life. After two years, He began to retreat from the limelight to pour Himself into this future management team. One day, He asked them a simple question: "Who do people say I am?" (Mark 8:27).

The disciples listed several options that the masses had suggested for the true identity of Jesus. Then Jesus asked, "Who do *you* say I am?" Peter answered, "You are the Christ, the Son of the living God" (v. 29; see also Matt. 16:15-16).

Bingo! Peter got it right. The disciples were clear in their understanding when everyone else's was fuzzy. So Jesus began to explain why He had come. In restating His mission, He told the disciples that soon He would head up to Jerusalem where He would suffer many things at the hands of the religious leaders. Finally, He would be killed; but three days later, He would be raised again to life.

Peter didn't like what he heard, so he pulled Jesus aside. I can just hear Peter telling Jesus off. He probably said something like, "Wait a minute, Jesus! We've got to talk. Do You know what's going to happen if You go through with this? People won't want to follow You. This makes no sense. Just drop it and let's come up with another plan."

Listen: If Peter could treat Jesus like that, don't be surprised if some people are out of step with you over your mission. In fact, some folks will think you are wacko. Some will challenge you over your position. So don't depend on the encouragement of the gallery to continue your quest; support may not be there.

Once you sell out to a life purpose, you also may acquire an enemy who would like to thwart your effectiveness. He is the enemy of all those who live in keeping with God's overall purpose for the planet. His earliest name was Lucifer; his actions in opposition to God established for him a new identity—he was rebranded as Satan. He is often referred to as "the devil." He's a real spiritual personality who firmly opposes all that God plans to do in the cosmos.

The devil was involved in the tiff between Peter and Jesus. Jesus recognized that and pointed out to Peter that Satan himself had stimulated his challenge to Jesus' mission: "Get behind me, Satan! You are a stumbling block to me; you do not have in mind the things of God, but the things of men" (Matt. 16:23). Inadvertently, Peter had begun to mouth the message espoused by the other side: "The mission wasn't worth the cost!"

Jesus is saying, "You are out of step, not Me. I'm in step with God; you're in step with men." If you're in step with God, and you have a sense of mission, you may find yourself at odds with some around you.

Another important thing to remember: Initially, Jesus didn't announce His mission to the world. He only revealed it to a select group of people. We might be wise to do the same.

His Commitment to Mission Increased His Impact on People

Jesus headed to Jerusalem knowing that it was His final trip on earth. The disciples were astonished that He had such a clear purpose in returning to the city (see Mark 10:32). Again He took the Twelve aside and told them what would happen. Still they continued to follow Him.

It helps to understand that these disciples were not a rag-tag bunch of transients with nothing better to do. They had jobs. They were in midlife. They had successful careers. They had investments in capital expenditures essential to their business.

One day, years before, Jesus had come along and said, "If you guys are smart, you will walk away from what you're doing and join up with Me." He didn't offer them stock options. He didn't offer them management positions. He just said, "Come with Me." And they came. Why? His was a magnetic personality, and at least part of that magnetism was that He was on a mission. They didn't understand the mission, but they were mightily impressed by it.

We can look at men and women over the course of history and find that those who were on a mission, even a destructive one, drew loyal followers to their cause.

> We can look at men and women over the course of history and find that those who were on a mission, even a destructive one, drew loyal followers to their cause.

How do you explain Mother Teresa? Or Osama bin Laden? Righteous or evil, there's something compelling about someone who knows what he or she is out to do. People long to be part of a cause greater than they are, and they're often prepared to sacrifice much to join in following a leader who can take them somewhere.

If you want to increase your impact on society, and you want a following of people who can't seem to spend too much time around you—be a person who knows where he or she is going. You will attract people, and they'll follow.

His Dedication to Mission
Brought Glory to God

I can't get over how Jesus, the night before He died, said He had completed His mission. So many people I meet never feel they get done with their work. Some feel like they've never even started. When they're near death, they say, "I'm not done; there's so much more I need to do."

But here's Jesus saying He's finished His task, and He's been dedicated to it for just over three years. He says to God, His Father, that this work has brought glory to God. God gets the credit for what was accomplished.

It's tempting to pen a quick purpose statement for your life based on some deeply embedded truth you tucked away in your youth. For many people raised with a religious background, a statement of belief found within the Westminster Catechism—a key part of some church training programs—declares an answer to the question:

> The chief end of man is to glorify God and enjoy him forever. . . .

"Purpose statement?" somebody asks. "Sure, I've got one! My purpose is to glorify God. Simple."

That's good, but it's not enough. Jesus said He had accomplished that end, but He achieved it through a specific means.

Notice what Jesus said. He didn't say that He had glorified God through His belief system. He didn't do it through His faith. He didn't even do it through His tender heart. He said He glorified God by completing the work—the mission—God had given Him to do.

This takes it down to a practical level. Jesus didn't just talk a good story; He didn't glorify God only in theory. He figured out what God wanted Him to do and He did it. I can get my arms around that, can't you?

His Mission Was Completed When His Earthly Life Was Over

While hanging on the cross, Jesus uttered these words: "It is finished."

There's a special word for finished. You've experienced it whenever your to-do list is completed and you've done all that was expected of you. You feel it when you clear out that inbox of emails that has been piling high on your digital desktop. That word is "peace."

Here's a man on a cross, suffering in agony for your failures in life, bearing the burden of all the combined failure of humankind. And He's at peace!

Why? He was done; finished. His mission was completed.

How would you like to define your target so clearly that you know your mission is complete when you pass away? I submit to you that you'll never be able to say it if you haven't figured out what your purpose is. For what purpose are you here? Is it to launch a new net-based enterprise? Move more product? Take your company public? Secure more contracts, employ more people, build bigger buildings, spend more time on the freeway, get bills passed? What lame targets have loomed large in your past life only to become inconsequential victories once they were achieved?

For what purpose are you here? The average answer to that question isn't big enough to define life. Yet, I'm just radical enough to believe that every man and woman reading this book has a mission. But for the most part, my observation is that those missions remain undiscovered.

Nineteenth-century architect and urban planner Daniel Burnham, who built America's first skyscraper, once said, "Make no little plans. There's nothing in little plans to stir men's blood. Make big plans. Once a big idea is recorded, it can never die."

Don't define your life in inconsequential terms. It won't carry you very far. If your life is not in line with a grand purpose, there is no good reason to go about it. There is no good reason to answer the bell for the next round when you've been beat up in the last one.

So, what do you do? How do you find your mission in life? If you're interested, Jesus left a great mission. And He has invited you to be a part of it.

] 5 [

YOUR LIFE PURPOSE
STATEMENT

By now, I hope you're beginning to get the drift: A personal purpose statement is as important to your life as a set of accurate blueprints is to the erection of a quality building. Many lives are under construction without a plan, but the best ones are built with design in mind.

For more than 20 years, I had tried one time-management system after another, seeking to bring order to my life. Though they varied in layout and color, they all shared a common assumption: an orderly life results from maintaining orderly days.

Nobody was more committed to a calendar than I was. My calendar was more likely to accompany me than my wife. Everything was written down. I was married to my schedule. If a disciplined life was an effective life, I had to be the most effective guy in town. Right?

Wrong! Here's an example of my typical experience:

Ring-ring. "Hello?"

"Hey, Bob? This is Bill. I'd like to talk to you about the cause I mentioned when I ran into you at the club last week. Are you free for lunch on Tuesday?"

I shuffle papers and reach for the calendar book (this was years before schedules were kept on your smart phone!). Check Tuesday: all clear for lunch.

"Yes, Tuesday is free."

"Great! I'll pick you up at your office about noon. I know you'll want to be involved in this thing when you hear about it."

Am I free? Are you kidding? Talk about out of control; I was free unless someone else had already nailed me. Sure, I was getting a lot of my own line items on the calendar, but a huge block of my time was leaking out to other people and their appeals.

On one particularly hectic day, I decided to see how many of my week's activities had been determined by me and how many were scheduled by someone else's request. The answer sobered me immediately. Half of my discretionary time was being scattered to the wind under the control of people who happened to have my phone number.

Clearly, this was unhealthy. Although I never missed an appointment, and my days were ordered with precision—chock-full of random activities—my life was out of control.

My working philosophy began to break down. String seven disciplined, disjointed days together into a week, hook 52 of these weeks together in succession and that was supposed to be a meaningful year?

One recent January, I lunched with three CEOs. I asked each of them to describe what he considered the most important accomplishment or significant contribution he had made during the prior year. They looked at each other in silence, unable to identify one major achievement from the last 12 months of their lives. They felt the same emotional upheaval I had experienced a few years before.

Here's the confusion:

Well-managed days do not result in a well-managed life.
Well-managed days are the result of a well-managed life.

The fact is, you can be disciplined without being deliberate. But God will not hand you a Medal of Honor just for making it to all of your appointments on time.

....

You can be disciplined without being deliberate. But God will not hand you a Medal of Honor just for making it to all of your appointments on time.

....

What follows in the remainder of this chapter is a process to help you formulate a statement of purpose for your life. Your personal statement of purpose can become the foundation for directing how you manage your time, energy and resources. It is worth whatever it takes you to conceive, carry and birth it.

Let's use the construction analogy one more time. You are far enough along in life that many elements needed to state your purpose are already in place. You aren't starting with a bare lot, devoid of construction materials. You're standing on a piece of prime property—the remaining years of your life—with grant deed in hand. Many architectural items already sit in crates on the site, waiting unpacking and installation. You have a toolbox filled with specific implements. Workmen stand by, expecting direction on how to proceed. It seems you have everything you need to begin—except the plans.

It's up to you to draft the working drawings. However rudimentary they are, it is essential to have something from which to work. It won't suffice to say, "Let's build a house." If no specifics are forthcoming, chaos is only hours away.

A line from *Alice in Wonderland* sure fits here: "If you don't know where you're going, any road will get you there." Even though the pressure's on to get to work, you must take a break and take inventory.

"But what should I draw?" you ask. First, you need to consider and take into account a number of fundamental elements. The nature of your piece of property is important: How big is it? Where is it located? What are its characteristics? Your own interests are at issue too: What kind of house do I want? With what style am I most comfortable? How much space do I need? The materials already gathered require examination: Do they fit together? Are there enough materials to do the job? Do I have working materials that don't belong together?

You also need to sort through the toolbox: What special implements are there? Are the workmen trained to use all of the devices at my disposal? How about the workers: Are they really the right people to build this house? Are there enough? Too many? Will they work together well?

Since you serve as both architect and superintendent, you are keenly interested in creating a good design.

In fact, since you'll be living in the place once it's built, you couldn't be more emphatic about the project and its successful completion!

Evaluating Your Life

Back to your life: You'll be the one living in it, and nobody else. Doesn't it make sense to spend the time necessary to produce the highest quality design possible? I believe God has placed some specific clues around you to assist in the process. In fact, it is His design you want to discover . . . the one that represents His maximum intent for your life. Anything less is to miss the mark of highest and best use.

So, let's look at the things unique to you that need to be considered. As we do, use the space provided to write down your observations and ideas. This will provide the information you need to formulate your life purpose statement.

1. Your Unique Gifts and Abilities

One thing that makes you special is the mix of abilities, both natural and spiritual, that God has assigned to you. That's the right word—"assigned"—because God says He chose your gifts and abilities just for you.

Did you ever wish you had someone else's abilities? Did you ever find yourself wondering why you couldn't do what someone else does so well? It's easy to focus on what we can't do in the light of what others can do, forgetting that we have unique capabilities as individual as our fingerprints.

On the natural level, we call these abilities *talents*. Some people have an uncanny intellectual capacity that baffles us. Others have the instinct to recognize great investments or business opportunities. In the sports arena, "natural athletes" wow us with their physical prowess. None of these examples can be traced to deliberate, willful choice on the part of the recipient. They were given this potential.

Certainly, two people who have been handed the same talents can come to very different ends, based on their willingness to apply themselves. But the basic inborn capacity is there through the sovereign decision of the Creator.

When we move to the spiritual arena, people who enjoy a personal relationship with Jesus Christ have received a special gift from God. The Bible calls these capabilities spiritual gifts, specifically selected and conveyed by God to members of his family (see Rom. 12:3-8; 1 Cor. 12:1-11). Broadly speaking, these gifts are either communication gifts or serving gifts. Within those wide parameters are numerous, highly valuable endowments that make participation in the work of God something vastly better than a dubious exercise in volunteerism. For the enlightened folks who recognize and understand their gifts, service becomes deeply enjoyable and highly effective.

....

For the enlightened folks who
recognize and understand their gifts,
service becomes deeply enjoyable
and highly effective.

....

As we move through each element of a complete purpose statement, I want to make sure this doesn't become theoretical. So I will demonstrate by using the process Cheri and I went through as we prepared our purpose statement.

As Cheri and I evaluated what gifts and abilities set us apart, we both recognized that people around us already thought our communication skills were our most identifiable distinctives. Though we could do other things well, we did these things the best.

This was a key piece in our puzzle. Bottom line: We discovered that God could use us to teach other people practical truths about life. Of all of the things we could do in our lives, this was the most rewarding.

Now take a look at yourself. Why did God give you unique capabilities? Did He intend you to store them, or to use them center stage? In forging a personal purpose statement, a foundational starting point is to determine your gifts and talents. To maximize your life experience you should use these to the fullest extent.

Take some time to think through your natural abilities. List the three that you feel are most likely to play a part in your future:

1. _____
2. _____
3. _____

Now, consider your spiritual gift(s). If you're not sure what your gifts are, read through the following passages found in the New Testament and jot down the gifts you think may describe you:

Romans 12:3-8:

_____
_____
_____
_____
_____

1 Corinthians 12:1-31:

_____

_____

_____

_____

_____

1 Peter 4:10-11:

_____

_____

_____

_____

_____

2. Your Unique Personal Passion

In the last quarter of the last century, an innocuous expression became popular: "Whatever turns you on!" People were granted license to pursue anything as long as it "turned them on." In a misguided way, this encouraged people to pursue their passions, though in those years, passions often went away.

Somewhere along the line, the "turned on" generation dropped its passion and forgot to go back and pick it up. Pragmatic reality and daily demands pushed passion off center stage as meeting quotas and paying down debt became the new reality.

I meet so many people who are living dreary lives of mere existence rather than energizing lives of passion. One man told me recently that the strongest drive that led him out of his marriage was a search to rediscover some passion for living.

Passion isn't a tawdry subject for followers of the Lord Jesus Christ; in fact, it is one of the characteristics that allows us to mirror the divine! God is the ultimate picture of passion; He does nothing without it! Jesus' passion drove His pursuit of His purpose.

I spent an hour one evening talking with a young single man struggling to define his purpose. When I asked about his passion, he immediately began to relate his deep concern and love for kids hospitalized with life-threatening illnesses. He told me how every evening, after work, he spent hours on the oncology floor of the local children's hospital. His eyes filled with tears as he recalled name after name of the boys and girls he befriended during their struggles with cancer or leukemia.

I asked the man if he hated to go to the children's hospital. He told me he loved it—he hated to see the kids suffer, but he loved to be there with them, to comfort them and be a friend.

The years that Cheri and I spent in business allowed us to cultivate and nurture friendships with many other individuals and couples. Many had gone through difficult times, and we watched as they struggled with issues and challenges from which we had been protected through our faith. We both felt a burden to help these friends, knowing that help was available through the faith we shared. Our passion was to assist men and women within our leadership-level peer world through the resources of the Christian faith.

Recent surveys have probed the question of passion in numerous ways. One survey sought to discover the things that young adults valued enough to be willing to go to war for—in effect, the things for which they would die. The majority did not value a concept, a right, or an issue enough to risk their lives. Nothing for them was worth dying for.

Here's a thought to ponder: If you don't have anything worth dying for, do you really have anything that is worth living for?

When something so moves your heart and demands your energy that you'd do anything to make it happen, you're on the path to your passion.

I've discovered something interesting: People driven by passion are so rare and captivating that they tend to draw others to them. They become magnetic and infect others with their passion. People who have never been energized by anything become "kamikazes" for a leader with passion.

....

People driven by passion are
so rare and captivating that they tend
to draw others to them.

....

Randall Terry, the head of Operation Rescue, had a passion for saving the lives of unborn babies. His passion often has taken him to a jail cell, yet masses surrounded him, influenced by his passion.

Nelson Mandela, the head of the African National Congress, had a passion for dismantling apartheid in South Africa. His passion held him in a prison cell for decades, yet masses surrounded him, influenced by his passion.

Mother Teresa, the mercy-giver of Calcutta, had a passion for extending kindness in Jesus' name. Her passion kept her in a place devoid of comfort or ease. Yet, masses surrounded her, influenced by her passion.

The list could go on and on. People with passion have always drawn a crowd. They know what they want to see happen, and they're willing to invest everything they have, even their lives.

How about you? Have you cultivated or discovered a passion? Is it planted in your heart and thriving through your life? In the space below, describe the cause or issue that raises your temperature and wins your loyalty:

_____

_____

_____

_____

_____

3. Your Unique Personality

This is just a guess, but I'll bet you are different from the people closest to you. It is often observed, "Opposites attract." We all tend to fall into relationships with others whose personalities are significantly different, albeit complementary, from our own.

It is an unusual marriage that finds two similar personalities together. If "we're as different as night and day" was the battle cry for dissolution, 99 percent of marriages would end up on the rocks. Thriving marriages recognize the high odds of big differences and celebrate them.

You are unique. Your personality is among your special distinctives, and there are no inherently "bad" personalities. Understanding who you are and how you are inclined is a big piece in the life-management puzzle.

Consider how much this affects your daily activities and your attitude toward them. As a result of your temperament:

- You may enjoy being with people, or you may prefer being alone.
- You may like living with risk, or you may need to feel secure.
- You may enjoy taking leadership, or you may want to follow.

- You may tend to focus on projects, or you may tend to focus on people.
- You may wish to create a movement, or you may look instead for your niche.

None of these differences is right or wrong; they are just differences. Hostility and relational stress often erupt when people try to change others into mirror images of themselves. They are often unaware of the foundational differences in individuals, or they think it is a matter of decision, subject to change.

My wife and I conducted a healthy exercise one day while stuck on an airplane with nothing to watch, eat or hear. I fished through my carry-on bag and found a book given to me by a friend. It was one of the insightful temperament evaluation books on the market. This was the first time that the two of us, together, had a chance to use an objective system to measure ourselves in contrast to the other.

What a profitable investment of time! We discovered, much to our amazement, that we are the way we are because that's the way we are. While the descriptions of our temperament types weren't exact expressions of our idiosyncrasies, they were close. Little things that had been big irritants for years were found to be unintentional and inborn. Imagine: She hasn't been doing *that* all these years just to bug me.

For example, in this summary we recognized that Cheri was, though an extrovert, less extreme in that definition than I am. That didn't mean she didn't like people, nor that I couldn't stand to be alone. It simply showed that there were times when she would choose to be alone, while I would—almost always—be happiest among others. She would much prefer to be with family, while I liked to invite a busload of friends. It would be easy for her to read my tendency as not wanting to be with her and our daughters, when it didn't mean that at all. It was simply an unconscious difference of orientation.

There are numerous resources available to perform that sort of self-evaluation. The results are valuable in providing a mirror of your temperament.

How does temperament relate to mission? Your statement of mission will not put you in a position outside of your constitutional makeup. God made you the way you are for a reason, and He wants to put you to work in a way that takes maximum advantage of your strengths, not in a way that painfully exhibits your weaknesses!

At the risk of sounding ego-driven, many people regard Cheri and me as fun to be with. No one would use the term "sedentary" when referring to us. Those who know me recognize my sense of humor to be a valuable aspect of my makeup. Cheri is adventurous; she's game to try just about anything. Both of us are comfortable in front of people and want to help them enjoy life a little more. While we have plenty of differences, our personalities are such that we are generally comfortable around people.

Nobody knows you like God does, and He loves the way you're made. Have you discovered the best parts of His design, as seen in your custom personality? If you have a sense of your particular traits, write a paragraph to describe yourself, using language that is intangible rather than tangible (focus on your personality, not your person):

_____

_____

_____

_____

_____

4. Your Unique Responsibilities

God takes some responsibilities in your life very seriously. You should too.

I've watched people get fired up about going on a mission to impact the world yet lose the race in the starting block. With their hearts set on people across the ocean—people they have never met—they violate their responsibilities to those they've known for years in their own house.

You carry around a unique set of connections that heaven considers your primary relationships.

- If you are married, you pack a lifetime linkage to another person. Everything you do has to be considered in light of that person and his or her needs.

- If you are a parent, you are charged with the task of raising your children to become independent, functioning adults.

- If you are a child of surviving parents, you carry an obligation to assure the life support of your folks like they did for you.

- If you are a Christian, you are your brother's keeper to the extent of your capacity to supply his needs from your abundance.

In an era of carefree lifestyles and flaky commitments, God sounds a somber note of fiduciary and relational responsibility. We are not free to plot our lives on a course that takes us away from the people who depend on us for life support.

This isn't a question of money alone; it includes attention to the emotional, social and spiritual needs of those in our care. We are to look after the whole person.

During our momentous weekend, Cheri and I reaffirmed our resolute commitment to marriage. Neither of us wrestled with whether we could somehow tank our commitments to one another in favor of some grand mission. Further, we knew that our lifetime impact would rise or fall based on our ability to deliver two healthy daughters to adulthood. Nothing in our life purpose statement could challenge these priorities for either of us.

Formalize for yourself the names of the people who are your dependents.

Spouse:

_____

_____

_____

Children:

_____

_____

_____

Parents:

_____

_____

_____

Others whom God might consider as dependent on you:

_____

_____

_____

_____

5. Your Unique Experiences and Education

Nothing is more fun than meeting someone by chance for the first time and discovering that you share some common history. Perhaps you were raised in the same region or competed against one another in the same athletic league or maybe you attended the same college or university. You may have known some of the same people or worked for the same large corporation during your freshman career period.

Exploring your similarities with someone is a fascinating way to begin a relationship, but don't go overboard. You'll never find anyone who has exactly the same résumé you have. Even the best of friends who commit themselves in their youth to stick together through thick and thin get separated. The winding road of human experience just doesn't seem wide enough for two to stay together.

As you review the road map of your life, what do you discover? All of us have spent some time in backwater experiences we would never want to repeat, but we carried away mementos that we still find useful.

The quantity and quality of your education and experience (I have a hard time separating the two) is not only a result of where you've been and what you've done, but also how you've invested in where you've been and what you've done. Others could have shadowed you through life until now and arrived destitute.

Beyond our academic credentials, we all acquire an extensive list of experiences and accomplishments. We have been able to do things that others deem successful. My years of business and career attainment have won me the right to be heard by people who highly regard such things. Cheri has won the respect of full-time homemakers and professional women alike. For all of us, before too long in life, our accomplishments exceed our degrees; we find we have something to say, and people are willing to listen.

Your education and experience are priceless; you've spent the time since your birth purchasing both. What you are today, and what you have to offer tomorrow are, at least partially, the result of your investments in education and experience.

What are your best assets when you review your background? How are you a better person today as a result of where you've been and what you've done? Often, people don't perceive the value of their experiences until later in life. Time and perspective allow them to discover the truly meaningful moments of their younger years.

> Often, people don't perceive the value
> of their experiences until later in life.
> Time and perspective allow them to
> discover the truly meaningful moments
> of their younger years.

Ted has learned this lesson. Many years ago, too-rapid expansion and weak local management forced his multistate business into involuntary bankruptcy. Although this was a deeply humbling experience for a businessman of high integrity, Ted refused to let this incident blot his background. He doggedly continued to repay the firm's obligations from his personal resources, despite being relieved of personal responsibility by the courts.

Today, Ted has managed to repay every creditor. Moreover, he has used the lessons learned through this experience to deepen his personal resolve and develop his character. His ability to counsel and advise other men and women in similar difficulties is greater today because he made the best of a dreadful situation. He has taken his experience and maximized its value.

Part of the challenge here is to see your credentials in light of the opportunities they offer instead of the restrictions they impose. The "because I studied medicine, I have to be a doctor for the rest of my life" mindset will give you all of the options of a prisoner on death row (though better paid). Your background is your collection of assets, not a series of chains! If your experiences don't increase your options, you are allowing them to control your future rather than energize it.

Our nation's history has been enriched by people whose education and early career were simply opening acts for their ultimate performance. Ronald Reagan didn't retire from acting; he simply refused to retreat to a country club and chose instead to move from leading man to world leader, and navigate through the closing days of the Cold War.

Bill Gates built the computer operating system that ushered in the digital age and the personal computer; it made him one of the world's wealthiest men. Yet, his billions were not a ticket to personal indulgence: his wealth is funding his initiatives to change the world through entrepreneurial philanthropy.

Dave Dravecky was a major-league baseball pitcher when his season was interrupted with cancer in his pitching arm. He took leave to deal with the condition, and then staged a comeback that had fans on their feet. While on the mound, the world watched as his upper arm snapped, taking away his athletic career and, ultimately, his arm. That unwelcome intrusion opened the door for his post-career ministry with people confronted with cancer and other life-threatening disease. His amputation removed his arm but created a Kingdom service pathway that gives his life expanding impact.

Nobody will ever have the exact mix of lessons and life that you bring to the table. You are an expert in the arena touched by your life. How does your expert status in that area increase your capacity for contributing to significant things?

Take a few minutes to reflect on your life experiences. Don't just list your alma maters. Think about what you've learned, not where you've gone for the lessons. If knowledge is power, where are the concentrations of power in your life history? What have you learned that sets you apart from others? Describe your resource of knowledge in an autobiographical paragraph:

_____

_____

_____

_____

_____

For many people, where you've been and what you've done say more than anything else. What is your story? How are you set apart by life? What experience do you have that was worth the investment? Create another paragraph that tells your story from this perspective:

_____

_____

_____

_____

_____

_____

6. Your Unique Network

Twenty years ago, networks were nothing more than a group of broadcast stations under common control. Today, networks are flesh and blood. Rich people are still the ones who control networks, but these networks are alive.

Who do you know? Have you ever analyzed your network of relationships? How many people, really, do you know? Funeral directors have a good idea how to answer that question. Most mortuaries are designed around a funeral chapel that seats 250. This is not a chance determination; statistically, most people are in a network no larger than that. It is probable that no more than 250 souls will feel compelled to attend your funeral service.

We're talking about more than just Facebook friends. Casual bystanders are hardly the same as in-the-trench comrades. Networks are not the sum total of email addresses in your contact list: it's the short roster of those who would leave a meeting to return your text with a phone call to your mobile number.

If you are like most folks, you didn't recruit the people who will sign the book at your memorial service. Extended family members, people from work, neighbors who happened to buy the house across the street, the people who worked with you on committees—these are the faces that will greet your eulogizers. Unless, of course, you've done something to build that list intentionally.

You can influence this list. You can decide whether you want that number to be larger or smaller, and you have ultimate control over who makes up that group, whatever size you choose.

The majority of us know only those people whom we have happened to meet on our way through life. We didn't try to remember them; they just kept running into us along the way and it was easier to archive their names for next time than it was to keep asking who they were. Social contact grew out of this consistent interaction. Friends became friends because of activity in common, nothing more. Most of us accept random selection for the most significant relationships of our lives.

There is a proactive minority, however. Watch out for them, they're really different! These are people who think and talk about the kinds of men and women they want to know, and then they go on safaris to find them. They think nothing of calling a perfect stranger (the more perfect the better) and brazenly introducing themselves: "Hi, you don't know me, but I would like to change that." They solicit the friends they want listed on their schedule of personal assets.

Whichever kind of person you are, you have a network. It may be your network by accident, or it may be your network by choice. The nature of your network affects your mission. Who you know can radically affect the course of your life.

....

The nature of your network affects
your mission. Who you know can radically
affect the course of your life.

....

At Christmas time, you scratch your head to list all the names, intimate and distant, that you want to spray with your greeting cards and catching-up letters. In this next exercise, you'll need to think harder. We're not going for quantity here, but rather for quality. The question is not, "How many people do you know?" but rather, "Who do you know that is most strategic?" List the 10 people who are most integral to the quality of your life, both now and in the future. These are the 10 individuals you definitely want to maintain access to in the future.

_____

_____

_____

_____

_____

_____

_____

7. Your Unique Resources

A wise man once said that a person's life does not consist of the abundance of his possessions. He was right. That is not to say, however, that tangible resources have no impact on your life. The opposite is probably more accurate.

What you own says tons about you. The same sage said that your heart and your resources usually travel together. You put your money into the areas about which you are passionate. If you really believe in something, you will commit yourself to tangible expressions that include your most prized possessions.

Two people with identical gifts, temperaments, experiences and relationships can pursue substantially different missions in life because they are worlds apart in the area of resources. There is a serious and curious reason why that is true. There is evidence that the assets you hold and manage were placed in your hands intentionally, by God, and He plans for you to use them to advance His agenda, not yours.

That's a bold statement, but it needs to be said. I have often heard people state that a particular item is a blessing from God for something they did. That's a nice idea, but it doesn't hold water. God isn't passing out rewards yet; that comes later, in heaven. Between here and there, God is investing His assets with His people to be used purposefully for Him.

If above-average assets are under your control, you need to think seriously about some significant questions:

- Did God have a hand in your accumulating these resources?
- Has God had a part in your retaining those resources?
- Are there others you know who have worked as hard as you have, or harder, and not received what you have?
- If your possessions really belong to God and not to you, would He be happy with the way you are using them today?
- Does your financial plan reflect His ownership and His investment objectives, or does it reflect your own?

Even a cursory reading of the New Testament demonstrates that the person with above-average financial resources has a decidedly greater responsibility before God than the less-endowed person.

One way to avoid the onus associated with this issue is to disavow existence of the problem: "What? I'm not rich!" Any English-speaking resident of a Second World country whose income is at or above the median for his area is rich according to global standards. So accept the mantle. Better to act rich and not be, than to be rich and fail the test of faithfulness.

Cheri and I managed a generous income during our years in business, and we successfully controlled our lifestyle during that period. We avoided consumer debt and were working toward retiring the mortgage on our family home. One of our greatest assets was the lack of debt, something unusual among people of our generation, then and now. Further, we made it a practice to live on less than we made and had worked to increase our financial support for causes we believed in. So our lives were fairly simple in comparison to a majority of our professional peers. This provided us a fair amount of freedom because we didn't require all of the money I was capable of making. That was to significantly impact our life purpose statement.

What are your unique resources? What do you have that most of the world doesn't? There are lots of folks among your acquaintances who don't know you well but talk about you on the basis of what you have rather than what you are. In the space below, write down the things you possess that are most likely to be noted by these people:

8. Your Unique Allegiance

Bob Dylan flirted briefly with Christianity during the flexible middle years of his adult life. During that time, he released a number of songs with strong messages. One of them challenged listeners to accept this hard fact: *You gotta serve somebody.* There are no "free agents" in life. All of us are subservient to somebody. Dylan recognized only two options—from his lyrics, *we can serve the devil or we can serve the Lord.*

Actually, one of those options has almost unlimited subsets. You may think you are extending your loyalty to some seemingly noble cause or ideology, but if it's anything other than the Lord Jesus Christ, you have the wrong master. Jesus said it this way:

> No one can serve two masters ... Either he will hate the one and love the other, or he will be devoted to the one and despise the other (Matt. 6:24).

Your life is either pointed toward the King of heaven and His agenda, or it is pointed somewhere else. Any direction other than toward God is a move away from Him.

....

Your life is either pointed toward
the King of heaven and His agenda, or it
is pointed somewhere else.

....

Why is this important? When you hammer out a personal statement of purpose, you have to know where it's headed. If you claim to offer your homage to Jesus Christ, your purpose must find itself within His larger purpose for His Kingdom. If you are not allied with God through personal submission, quite frankly, any direction is equally viable. It doesn't matter which way you're going, it's a short-term trip, anyhow. But for the person tracking with God's purpose, this life is a warm-up for the main event!

Both Cheri and I are committed to the same Master. We each entered into a life-changing relationship with Jesus Christ during our youth. We feel no conflict over our individual expressions of submission to His lordship. In our Palm Desert summit, this was an easy conclusion: We were prepared to live out our lives for His benefit. In the process, we would find our own benefit.

The last great question from this list is the biggie: *Where is your unique allegiance?* Only two choices are possible; on which side of that divide have you chosen to be?

Managing Your Life

We're now ready to look at the finished life purpose statement. Years ago, Cheri and I laid out our discoveries about who we were and what we had available to us. The result was the following purpose statement:

> **Our life purpose** is to manage ourselves, our family and our resources in a way that will allow us to cause biblical life-change in business and professional men and women by teaching the timeless Word of God, to the glory of God.

We have since discovered dozens of subsets and footnotes that spring from this simplified statement. But for more than three decades, it has served to direct our decisions, and it looks like it will continue to take us through the remaining course of our adult lives.

Since that weekend in Palm Desert, Cheri and I have had many opportunities to teach friends and colleagues how to develop their own life-purpose statements. Here are some of theirs. Most are single-career or dual-career couples who are active in business as a profession.

Our life purpose is to live a life that is so reflective of Christ dwelling in us that it will impact and communicate Christ's message of life-change to our family, our community and as many other people as God directs to us, and to stretch to take hold of the future that God has for us, to the glory of God.

Our life purpose is to enrich the lives of our family, friends and those within our circle of influence by introducing and encouraging an approach to living centered around Jesus Christ, for the glory of God.

Our life purpose is to be sensitive to those around us who are lost and that through seeking and building relationships we might influence decisions for Christ, while staying grounded in God's Word, in the Church and in the fellowship of Christian friends, for the glory of God.

Our life purpose is to live a godly lifestyle, to know and understand God intimately, to bring as many people to faith in Christ as God allows, to equip and encourage Christians to do the same, and to generously support those who share this purpose, to the glory of God.

All of the eight areas we've covered represent distinguishing characteristics that make you different from everyone else. If you have thought these through and filled in the blanks, you have described a person (if you are married, a couple) who is set apart from every other individual on earth.

Your purpose—your overarching mission in life—will be a natural pursuit for the wonderfully made, divinely designed individual you are. You are probably closer right now to answering the "Why am I here?" question than ever before.

Success for you is ultimately defined by your own sense of having pursued your unique purpose in life. The personal distinctives you have articulated in this section are the basis for drafting a life-purpose statement. Clarifying your purpose is a process that begins with the first draft and continues through the course of the rest of your life.

Your statement of life purpose should answer the question, "Why do I exist?" It is more specific than simply saying, "My life purpose is to glorify God." That is true for every person. It is true, but not unique. How do you glorify God? That is the question your statement should answer.

On the night of His betrayal, Jesus prayed to His Father and expressed this truth: "I have brought you glory on earth by completing the work you gave me to do" (John 17:4). That's the goal you should have for yourself as well: to complete the work God has given you to do on earth, and thus bring Him glory. How heartbreaking to think you could stand before God someday and admit that you never took the time to discover the work He gave you to do, and then failed to do it.

As you write your life-purpose statement, here are two practical guidelines to keep in mind:

- Begin by listing all of the words, phrases and thoughts that seem to best describe the focus of your life.

- Continue simplifying your thoughts until they form one nontechnical sentence that anyone can understand.

It's now time to write out your own purpose statement. Take whatever amount of time is necessary to complete the following statement:

My life purpose is to . . .

_____

_____

_____

_____

_____

_____

_____

_____

_____

_____

_____

. . . for the glory of God.

] 6 [

Living on Purpose

By this point, you have either taken the time to think through the elements of the purpose statement and have created a first-generation prototype for yourself, or you're waiting to see what else I've got to say before you take on any homework assignments.

Whichever approach you've selected, I hope you agree that the whole idea is intriguing. Interpersonal discussion seldom lands on the subject of life purpose. If we don't talk about it, it's doubtful we'll be driven to think about it or, more importantly, do anything about it.

People who call a time-out to formalize their marching orders don't generally go around telling everyone they meet how they've chosen to live. It's more likely that they are going about the business of living. The difference is that they have figured out which way they want to move . . . and they're moving. You may know some people who fit this profile. You've determined that something is subtly different about their manner, but you haven't put your finger on what it might be.

Let me give you some clues to help you recognize purpose-driven people:

- They are selective about the areas in which they choose to get involved. They aren't against what other people are doing, but they don't get over-committed to multiple projects. They have a rationale for deciding where they devote their time.

- They appear to be more energized at the end of the day than at the beginning. Instead of dragging themselves out to the parking lot after sundown, they seem undaunted from days that drain the rest of the team.

- They look like they enjoy their successes more than others. They don't display the lack of lasting satisfaction that often follows an accomplishment. It almost seems that their achievements are leading to some bigger end, rather than ending up on a shelf to gather dust.

- They have enough time for all the things they are trying to do. They aren't complaining about their schedules or load; when they need time off, they go, and they return refreshed and in control.

- They don't have hundreds of acquaintances, but they are known to have some really special friends. They don't talk to everybody, but when they're talking to you, they're really there—you feel like you're the only other person on the planet when you're with them.

- They talk about the future with a sense of anticipation and destiny—as if they already know what it will be like, and it's exciting to consider arriving there to experience it.

- They portray no fear of the unknown—they don't seem to be flustered by things that upset those around them.

Purpose-driven people live with the benefits of a focused approach to life. They aren't like everyone else, but that doesn't bother them. They choose to be different in some of the most fundamental aspects of life.

This orientation to life is not without its difficulties. People who march to the tune of a different drummer stand out. People who stand out are not always commended. Accepting the potential of alienation is a necessary prerequisite, but it's worth that and more.

If you haven't yet written out a personal mission statement, I encourage you to do so now. (Even a bad one is better than none. As one hack put it, "A fool with a plan is imminently more effective than a wandering genius.") If you have written one, it is without value unless you assess what you do in light of that statement. This is the measuring stick by which you evaluate the things that require your energy, time and resources.

How do you respond to the person who calls with a worthwhile activity that requires your time?

I've found tremendous satisfaction in saying, "I'm excited about what you are doing, but it's not in line with my personal mission." It's interesting how quickly that caller hangs up; people don't know how to respond to a person who knows where he or she is going.

There are far too many people who "die" when they are 30 but aren't buried until they are 70. What a tragedy to live meaninglessly for decades! Fortunately, that waste is not necessary.

....

There are far too many people
who "die" when they are 30 but aren't
buried until they are 70.

....

If the idea of steering your life based on the dependable influence of a purpose statement is becoming attractive to you, you're ready to look at some of the ways such a life is expressed in the trenches. That's where we're heading with the second half of this book.

We move now from the foundational and theoretical aspects of this discussion to the practical arena. This concept of purpose-driven living works when it causes conscious change in the way you live out each day. Here are the six areas we will explore:

1. **Control:** By retaining authority over your allocation of time, energy and resources, you will progress toward your objectives rather than someone else's.

2. **Freedom**: By rejecting the entanglement of possessive influences, you will be able to speak, move and think in line with your life's purpose.

3. **Commitment**: By knowing the issues that are absolute, you will determine the essentials for allegiance to your cause; by protecting the values that define your life, you will illuminate your world.

4. **Availability**: By using an agenda rather than serving a schedule, you will have time for people who require compassionate attention even though they have no appointment.

5. **Focus**: By narrowing your scope of target and objective, you will succeed in achieving deep and lasting impact.

6. **Excellence**: By performing to your full potential, you will exceed the expectations of those who try to limit you to mediocrity.

As a living example, I want to use the life of Jesus. You'll never meet a better model of these six characteristics. This guy is amazing! In fact, the more you watch Him in action, the more you wish you could be like Him. Well, you can.

We're going to concentrate on events that transpired during the last three years of Jesus' life. His public work provides case study after case study for our consideration and review.

If you could somehow learn to live like Jesus—the perfect, paramount expression of what God intended men and women to be—you'd never want to turn back. And you'd never recover. Neither would your world.

That's our agenda for part two.

] 7 [

CONTROL

We're tempted to think that people who have "climbed the ladder" are in control of their lives. After all, how could they have made it that far without discipline? Too often, sadly enough, it just isn't so. Plenty of public examples demonstrate the point.

Senator Gary Hart was the front-runner for the 1988 Democratic presidential nomination. In one poll, he led his nearest competitor by an incredible 31 points. He appeared to be a man with substance. Not content merely to throw slogans at the American people, he constantly studied and proposed challenging new ideas in the areas of national defense and economics.

Hart admitted he was a man with a mission. His mother had convinced him of his special calling in life. He attended divinity school; and though he later dropped any religious vocation, he continued to feel a firm call to serve the common good in high public office.

But something drastically malfunctioned on his way to the White House. Rumors about marital infidelity had circulated for years, and perhaps in an earlier era such indiscretions would have been ignored. But when photographers spied him on a private yacht with actress and model Donna Rice, and caught him again meeting Rice at his Washington, D.C., apartment, the resulting public furor forced him to bow out of the race.

Senator Hart seemed baffled that the public would examine the private areas of his character and judge them more important than his stated policies and intentions for the presidency. It seemed to him like a double standard: while the public expressed ever-increasing freedom in the sexual arena, it also demanded higher qualities of honor and trust in its public officials.

Gary Hart was a man on a mission. But that mission, in and of itself, couldn't prevent his downfall. One of his campaign advisors said that his people assumed he *wanted* to be president and would discipline himself. They were right about what he wanted, but wrong in thinking that desire alone could generate the necessary discipline.

If we are to define total success in life, we must go beyond mission—as crucial as that is—and examine several essential qualities that allow a person to fulfill his or her mission. The first is *control*. By control, I mean consciously managing your allocation of time, energy and resources. Only with such control can you progress toward your objectives.

But what does this control look like? We can cite many examples of individuals who are highly successful in one sphere but totally undisciplined in others. We admire professional athletes, at least in part, because they demonstrate incredible discipline to train and become the best in their sport. But this control on the playing field doesn't necessarily translate to success in marriage, business or personal character. That's why we read about the tragedy of Pete Rose, one of major league baseball's all-time hit leaders, who couldn't control an addiction to gambling. Consider Charlie Sheen, a spectacularly successful sitcom actor who destroyed his life with addictions and eruptions. President Bill Clinton found his second term defined by the dalliances he allowed while in the Oval Office, and when required to defend himself and his inability to control his passions, he parsed the meaning of the word "is" in his impeachment deposition.

Only with control can you
progress toward your objective.

Examples of lack of control aren't always so spectacular. You might relate to the people who tell me they can't sustain relationships because of their travel schedule and they feel they have no ability to influence it. Others depend on the use of caffeine and sleeping pills. I've sat in offices with men who keep a luxury car brochure in front of them. They believe life won't be meaningful unless they buy that machine . . . and it drives them to make more deals, at the cost of their relational availability to their families. Still others secretly crave those private moments when they can get another fix from pornographic websites, hoping their spouse never discovers their addiction.

Fortunately, we have the perfect model of a man with a mission who also managed to control every area of His life. Public acclaim could not control Him. After one remarkable day during which He healed many and gave powerful words of encouragement, He refused to heed the popular cry to spend more time with this adoring crowd. Why? He told His followers He had other villages to visit and other people to whom He had to preach. "That is why I have come," He said. He knew His purpose in life, and He didn't let popular opinion sway Him from His course.

We know, of course, that this man was Jesus Christ—the most perfect example of control the world has ever seen. He provides the benchmark against which to measure our lives. If you were to suggest the benchmark for a contemporary pianist, you might name the artist Yanni. For a professional quarterback, you might choose Eli Manning. But if you want a benchmark for a man with a mission who lived a controlled life, there is no one better than Jesus Christ. For 33 years, God lived on planet Earth in the body of a man. This man faced the same demands, experienced the same drives, confronted the same external forces that we battle today, yet He never allowed His life to get out of control.

Let's look at His remarkable life and see if we can learn any lessons about how to keep our lives under control.

Keep Your Appetites Away from the Wheel

One of the first things we learn about Jesus was how He handled temptation. After John the Baptist baptized Him, Jesus took off for the wilderness. After 40 days of fasting and prayer, the Tempter came and invited Jesus to use His power to turn stones into bread.

Now, there's nothing wrong with being hungry. If any of us had gone 40 *hours* without a meal, we would look for a place to load up. Jesus had every reason to be hungry after 40 days without food. And even more significantly, He had the power to do something about it; He could have changed the rocks into bread.

But He didn't do that. Instead, He said, "It is written: 'Man does not live on bread alone, but on every word that comes from the mouth of God'" (Matt. 4:4). Jesus was saying that He would be in control, not His appetites. While there's nothing wrong with eating, He wasn't going to let His hunger govern His resolve.

That's the temptation we all face. For the most part, our appetites are normal and legitimate. But problems develop when those appetites start to control our lives. When uncontrolled, those appetites can destroy us.

It's significant that Jesus resisted this temptation alone in the wilderness. That is where most of us have to win the battle. Today, more than ever, the control we exercise in private can significantly impact our life and mission.

Religious leaders struggle with this as much as anyone. Our generation has almost become numb to the crisis *du jour* offered as headlines every time another prominent Christian ministry leader is deposed by lack of control. Each story has its own unique and sordid details, but they all have a consistent theme: In the middle of a life dedicated to religious service, temptation came calling . . . and control was nowhere to be found.

Appetites are universal; everyone has them, so we can all relate. The problem is never desire; the problem occurs when desire takes over and legitimizes the illegitimate. God made us with needs—physical, intellectual, spiritual, relational—and He is never against those needs being served in appropriate ways. But when desire becomes demanding, those once-wholesome desires can become our master, and we lose when we relinquish the control over desire that is critical to sustain and protect.

Jesus never succumbed to His appetites. He was not mastered by His desires; He exhibited the power that control gave Him—*and us*—against temptation.

Schedule Sufficient Time for Rest and Relaxation

Many people in the twenty-first century workplace no longer punch a time clock. We're fast becoming a "Free Agent Nation." The new independent contractor chooses when to start and when to stop. His or her workday is defined by projects and accomplishments rather than by hours and timecards. This is especially true for those who have attained the great American dream of working for themselves.

A few years ago, I conducted an informal survey among small business owners. One of the areas of inquiry concerned vacation habits. Most of these men and women had left positions with other firms to blaze their entrepreneurial trail into the future, on their own. At their previous employment, they had enjoyed an average of three weeks of vacation each year. They told me that one of the motivations for starting their own business was the chance to free up more leisure time. "When you're the boss," they told themselves, "you can be gone more." They wouldn't be hindered by personnel policies that limited their freedom.

My findings were humorous but sad. On the average, these independent entrepreneurs had been on their own for about five years. During that time, none had ever taken more than two weeks of vacation in any given year. And none of them had been gone for more than one week at a stretch in the previous year. Despite their original intent, they didn't believe they could be gone any more time than that. The very move that was supposed to increase their opportunities for rest instead increased the need for a break while reducing the supply of time to get away.

Jesus faced that same tension. He was inundated by the crowd's needs. From dawn to dusk He faced demands from people. It was enough to make anyone tired. Jesus recognized that and did something about it—both for Himself and His associates.

At one juncture, Jesus sent the 12 disciples out on a mission trip. When they returned, Jesus saw that they were both enthusiastic and exhausted, but crowds still pressed in on Him so much that there wasn't even time to eat. So Jesus said, "Come with me by yourselves to a quiet place and get some rest" (Mark 6:31).

To translate into today's vernacular, Jesus was saying, "Guys, the fact that the phones are ringing constantly and the schedule is jammed full is no reason to say we can't get away. If we need to rest, then we're going to go and rest."

Jesus did this throughout His ministry. He frequently escaped from the crowds and found a quiet place in the wilderness to pray. This quiet time was essential. It was the way He kept perspective, kept control over His schedule and recognized His priorities. He knew how important it was to keep His batteries charged . . . and He knew how to top them off.

Some people find this time early in the morning or late at night. They take a few minutes every day to pray, read the Bible and meditate. We need this kind of time daily. In addition, we need longer stretches away from the hustle and pressures of our careers.

You can sense it when you're with people: they're physically present, but they are running on empty. You may even frequently notice it about yourself. Are you exercising the control that keeps your gauges at or near "full?"

Maintain the Right to Select
Your Associates

One of the important news stories after a president gets elected is the naming of his cabinet and other key posts. The script is reenacted every four years, with new names filling in the blanks. Going into the major party conventions, the candidate for president has been determined in the primaries and the pick for vice president has been named to round out the ticket. All hands assemble on deck to put their party's picks into the White House the following January.

Soon after the November election settles the dust, the next round of top-level vetting surrounds the key selections that will define the new power elite in Washington: the secretaries whose cabinet roles will complement the president's vision and execute the policies he promised in the campaign season.

Perhaps even more important than these highly visible appointments are the secondary level choices—the sub-cabinet-level officials, the under-secretaries—who will have primary roles in forming and executing policies of the new administration. Without these key players, the president would have little hope of achieving his agenda.

Choosing the right associates is as critical for us as it is for a new president. We see this very clearly in the life of

Jesus. One day, Jesus rode a boat across the Galilee Lake to a region called the Gerasenes. There he met a wild man who lived in caves and was so strong that he could break the chains the locals used to contain him. Jesus confronted this man and ordered the demons to depart from him. It must have been an incredible sight, for the people of the region were so afraid they begged Jesus to leave.

....

Choosing the right associates is as critical for us as it is for a new president.

....

As Jesus boarded His boat, the man who had been demon-possessed begged to go with Him. I can sympathize with this man's request; he wanted to spend time with this remarkable Person who had just freed him. But Jesus wouldn't hear of it. "Go home to your family and tell them how much the Lord has done for you, and how he has had mercy on you," Jesus said. (See Mark 5:19.)

Why did Jesus refuse this man's request? Would it have made that much difference, adding one more person to His team, especially someone so obviously grateful? The answer is found in the way He chose His associates. Earlier in His career, as Jesus gained popularity, He found Himself surrounded by more and more disciples. It was becoming unmanageable. Further, Jesus recognized that if He was going to accomplish His mission, He needed to spend quality time with a handful of men. He simply could not effectively train such a large group.

So one night, Jesus went off alone to a mountain and spent the entire night in prayer. The next morning, He called all of His followers together and chose 12 to be His disciples.

For the remaining years of His ministry, while He didn't ignore the multitudes, He concentrated on these 12 men. The point is clear: Jesus, after careful thought and prayer, chose 12 men He wanted around Him. They didn't choose Him.

You may be surrounded by people who have taken control of your life. They call you and dictate where you'll be tonight, what you'll do this weekend, what projects you will do next and how you will spend your casual hours. They have decided to influence, perhaps even direct, your life. You may have even attempted to explain it as unavoidable, telling yourself, "It comes with the turf."

If the people who occupy your life are people you did not choose to fill that role, your life is out of control. You're living under the direction of others. Jesus modeled a far different approach. He chose where His time would be spent. If someone had called Him on the phone and said, "We've got to get together right now," He might well have said, "Not necessarily." Do you realize that you don't have to accept every invitation and appointment?

Oh, great, you might be thinking, *this is my chance to get out of this marriage. I just wasn't thinking when I got into this relationship, and now I'm going to take control.*

Sorry, but no way. If you're involved in relationships with people by covenant (as in marriage), or by contract (as in a business situation), then you stick to your guns and fulfill your commitments in those relationships for the term of the agreement (and remember, by God's design for marriage, that's for life!).

In this context, I'm actually focused on those situations where you have accepted or created a responsibility that really isn't there. Let me give you an example.

I was talking recently with a business executive who was losing interest in her husband. There wasn't any glaring inadequacy, she just found herself examining him critically in private and becoming irritated over petty things. I asked what she thought might be driving her new attitude toward him.

Turns out, she had been lunching almost daily, and for some time, with some other professional women, and all three of the others had been divorced in the last five years. None of them had any good thing to say about their former husbands. She found herself unengaged in the conversations but quietly internalizing what she was hearing over lunch. She was comparing her life situation with that of the others around the table.

As we talked, she concluded that the benefits to be gained from her time with her friends were less valuable to her than the damage it was doing to her marriage. Any obligation she had to them was self-imposed. She needed to get control before her internal struggles turned openly damaging to her marriage.

It's easy to find yourself in those kinds of relationships. Perhaps there are people with whom you spend time who have the potential to keep you from being everything you could otherwise be. Have you avoided taking control of those types of friendships? Don't avoid it any longer!

Reject Any Advancement That Will Assure Your Decline

Not long ago, I was with a man who lost a close race for Congress. Since he lost by only a few votes, there was plenty of potential for remorse over what might have been. He, however, was not at all dejected; he was becoming increasingly glad for the loss. "Great legislators aren't necessarily great fathers," he told me. He saw that political victory might have brought personal defeat. For him, the emotional, adrenaline-driving work of Congress might not have been compatible with being an effective father to his pre-adolescent children.

It's a good thing this man didn't have to learn the lesson the hard way. This is one of the hardest things to realize: to see our limitations and decide not to exceed them. Recently, I met with a friend who is in senior management for a billion-dollar company. He was lamenting the personal cost of his high-level position. He is seriously considering going to the CEO with a request to move one rung *down* the corporate ladder. Why? He finds himself envious of friends whose lesser positions grant them a higher quality of life. He said he's been had by the allure of the boardroom, and now he wants out.

How do we know whether to accept, or even pursue, a higher position? The answer goes back to our sense of mission. Unless we know our purpose in life, we don't know our limits. Even when we know our mission, the temptation inevitably comes to compromise it; and often the compromise may be compelling because of its apparent superior value. Control means knowing whether that advancement fits with our mission, and acting accordingly.

Jesus faced this temptation. He had just preached to a huge crowd—perhaps as many as 20,000 people (5,000 men, plus women and children). The people were hungry, and Jesus performed one of his most memorable miracles. With a boy's lunch of five loaves and two small fish, he fed the whole mob. Not only that, but the disciples gathered 12 baskets full of leftovers. (See Mark 6:30-34.)

The people were impressed. They quickly saw all kinds of possibilities. Jesus would make the perfect king! He would overthrow the Roman occupiers! With Jesus as king, they would never go hungry! They also suspected, however, that Jesus wouldn't accept a formal request, so they laid plans to force Him to be their ruler. But Jesus knew what was happening; He dismissed the crowd and immediately withdrew to a mountain to be alone.

My friend Bill received a call from "The Man" in a Fortune 500 company. It was the last person he expected to hear from. What was more, the call was to offer him a position he'd worked for all of his professional life: "We want you to take over our Minneapolis office." Implied in that invitation was the chance for corporate management on the highest level a few years down the road.

Isn't it obvious what Bill should do? As some might say, "it's a no-brainer." Why even pray about it? Isn't God's will obvious here?

But Bill did pray about it. While this was the position he'd hoped for, the job meant moving his family 2,000 miles. He and his wife were just starting to see significant results from their investment in the lives of men and women they'd befriended over the years in the community where they had established their relational neighborhood. The career advancement would uproot them from that field. It would take years to reestablish the kind of relationships they now enjoyed. The more he prayed and thought about the opportunity, the more he realized it wasn't right for him.

I know many people with Fortune 500 companies who have lived in places they never even knew existed. Most of them would never go back to these places, but they were necessary stops toward their ultimate objective. When the company said, "Jump," they answered, "How high?" They knew they might be forgiven once for refusing a move, but not twice. And yet for many of them, the advancement was not in their best missional interests.

That's the scenario here with Jesus. He recognized that a promotion to king was the worst thing He could do. In essence, he said, "You can keep this honor. That's not why I have come."

Mastering Your Life

While nothing is more convicting than examining the recent history of your life, there is no better way to stay on track with your mission. I suggest you call up your personal schedule for the last two weeks and review it in light of what you have read in this chapter about "control." Go through each line item in your calendar and put a number by each item where you have violated one of the four principles of control we've examined:

#1 Appetite-driven decision;
#2 Needed rest but kept on going;
#3 Gave time I could not afford to someone I would not choose;
#4 Enticed by position that isn't for me.

Once you've reviewed your calendar, go back and count the times each number is noted. The number with the highest score deserves your prompt attention.

] 8 [

FREEDOM

Mention the word "freedom" and many of us conjure up images of sexual revolution, unrestrained individuality, libertarian excesses run amok and alternative lifestyles.

Or, we become political and think of crowds assembled in public squares, calling for the ouster of unpopular governments. Freedom can quickly become a self-serving agenda, individually or collectively.

But that is not what freedom means for those involved in LifeMastery. For men and women with mission, freedom means rejecting the entanglement of possessive influences so that they are able to speak, move and think in line with their life's purpose.

Contemporary society fosters a subtle form of slavery. Though we believe we overcame that problem as a society some 150 years ago, it continues today in ways that we seldom seriously consider. The degree of impairment may vary, but the lack of personal freedom is rampant.

Just how free are you today? If you were to travel anywhere in the world and ask average people, "What is the most free place in the world to live?" most would answer, "America." Based on what they read and see on television, they are convinced that the United States is the land of ultimate freedom. You can wear what you want, eat anything you like, do whatever you please. There are no limits.

Of course, that picture is illusory. We only have to look at the statistics of people addicted to some mind-altering drug or lifestyle to know how untrue it is. But there is a more subtle form of bondage that many don't recognize.

The only thing more pitiful than a person who is a slave and knows it is a person who's a slave but thinks he is free. We in the United States live among a society of slaves.

> The only thing more pitiful than a person who is a slave and knows it is a person who's a slave but thinks he is free.

I visited a man in his high-rise office in one of the leading cities in America. From his desk he enjoyed a marvelous view of the city. The man worked for one of those companies where your elevator stop reflects the amount of power you have. Those who exit before you are underlings. The ones who stay on after you get off are called "Sir" or "Ma'am." This man's place in the pecking order was rising dramatically.

As we looked out the window into a beautiful plaza, I noticed some people sitting on the benches, in no hurry to go anywhere. I asked my friend, "How free do you feel?"

"Are you kidding?" he responded. "I've never before had the freedom I have now."

"Let me rephrase that." I pointed to the plaza, noting that some of the people there probably didn't have a home beyond the bench where they would lay their heads that night. "I would propose that some of those people down there are freer than you are."

My friend didn't believe me.

I said, "You know, the weather in Florida is incredible right now. Why don't you come with me and we'll spend a couple of weeks on the beach in Miami?"

"Now you're just making a hypothetical proposition," he protested.

"Let's pretend I'm serious. Do you want to go with me?"

"I'd love to, but I can't."

"Why not?"

He opened the calendar on his desk and showed me the plan for his immediate future designed by the people who could demand his time. His appointment schedule looked like the final days of a presidential campaign.

"How much notice would you need to be able to get away for two weeks?" I asked.

"Bob, I haven't had a two-week vacation in years," came the sad reply.

"Look down below. In that plaza right now, if I showed up with some prepaid tickets, I could get a busload of people to go with me to Miami. They're free to go now, and you're not. So who's more free?"

About this time, our allotted time was up. His next appointment was in the outer office (I knew, because his assistant had already come in to remind me that I was nearly finished). I'm afraid my friend felt better before I came than when I left. But the point was clear. He wasn't really free.

My point is not to say that freedom allows us to do anything we want when we want. Rather, the question is: Are you able to call the shots in your life, or are you living with chains wrapped around your leg?

The freest person who ever walked on this planet was Jesus. In fact, He said He came "to proclaim freedom for the prisoners" (Luke 4:18). To my knowledge, there is no record of Jesus ever visiting a prison. Certainly the freedom he proclaimed was for literal prisoners, as well, but I believe He also made this statement for people who were prisoners of daily life—prisoners of the things that controlled them.

In what ways was Jesus free? We can look at how He didn't worry about where He would sleep or what He would eat and drink. That's nothing much for you; you would say you don't worry about those necessities either. But Jesus didn't have a home to call His own, and often He didn't know where He would obtain His next meal. However, He never considered that to be a burden; rather, He was free to come and go as His mission demanded. For Him, there were no mortgage payments, no utility bills, no worrying about grocery shopping and meal planning.

Am I suggesting, then, that we follow this pattern? Should we walk away from our homes and forget about stopping at the grocery store? No. Rather, these things should not preoccupy us the way they often do. Instead, we should be free to concentrate on fulfilling our purpose in life. The person in bondage worries about how he will pay his bills. All of his credit cards are at the limit. He dreads the arrival of the mailman, who might bring another notice of overdue payment. He's constantly worried about how to get out of debt, and his only hope is that the MegaBall lottery ticket he bought when he filled his gas tank will be a winner. Certainly we would agree this person is not free.

Jesus demonstrated freedom for us in a number of ways. Let's look at four of them.

Keep Yourself Free from Ineffective Traditions

Motivational speaker Zig Ziglar once told about a family preparing to celebrate Christmas. John was home from the office and hanging around the kitchen. His wife, Mary, was scurrying around him as she prepared the ham for the oven. As part of her ritual, she cut off the end of the ham and set it aside. "Why did you do that?" John asked.

"That's the way my mom always did it," was her quick response.

Fortunately, Mary's mother was in the living room, so John—lacking any constructive role in the holiday get-ready routine—continued to pursue an explanation for the hacked-off ham. "Mom, why do you cut off the end of the ham?" he asked.

"I don't know," she answered. "I learned it from my mother."

Now John was really curious. He decided to call up Grandma in Indiana. After exchanging the necessary pleasantries, he asked, "Grandma, why did you always cut off the end of your ham before you baked it?"

There was a moment of silence before Grandma answered: "Because my pan was too short."

It doesn't take long before a reasonable response to a practical situation becomes a tradition. By the time a second generation enters the picture, armies can form to protect the sanctity of a practice that originally had significant pragmatic value but little or no continuing importance.

One day, Jesus had a run-in with some masters of tradition. They were called Pharisees, and they taught the law to the Jewish people. These teachers asked Jesus, "Why don't your disciples live according to the tradition of the elders instead of eating their food with 'unclean' hands?" (Mark 7:5).

Now, these men weren't talking about washing their dirty hands before dinner. They demanded that people perform a ceremonial cleansing anytime before they ate. Why? *Because the elders, the folks who lived in previous generations, had established that tradition.*

If you ever wanted to find a society where tradition was king, you couldn't do much better than first-century Israel. Jesus grew up in this culture, but see how He responded when challenged. He called the Pharisees "hypocrites" because they enforced human traditions while ignoring the commands of God. He didn't deny all tradition, but insisted that tradition without substance has no value.

....

Jesus didn't deny all tradition,
but insisted that tradition without
substance has no value.

....

Many people suffer from the same problem in America: Corporate public relations departments have shaped our lifestyle expectations and our values. Perhaps you remember when you graduated from school and entered the work force. At first, you offered bold and fresh approaches to problems, thinking this was the way to move up the ladder. After all, if you found a way to do things a better way, everyone would rise up and call you blessed . . . *right?*

Well, they do rise up, but "blessed" is not the word they call you. Perhaps you've pulled a few arrows out of your posterior; for example, you've been bruised by floating an idea that no one wanted to hear, even though you're convinced it's an improvement over the way it's always been done.

After you've heard the words "we've always done it this way" and you've had your nose broken a few times trying to change things, you finally give up. You decide you'll live within the confines of the traditional approach.

Jesus said He wasn't bound to ineffective tradition. He said he would do anything necessary to be effective. Tradition did not govern His methods; His mission did.

Don't Be Hindered by Unhealthy Relationships

Jesus was beginning to generate tremendous public acknowledgment. Crowds flocked to Him to hear Him speak and receive His healing touch. And how did His family feel about this? Not as you might expect. In fact, open hostility soon broke out from His brothers.

The four half-siblings of Jesus—the New Testament identifies them as James, Joseph, Simon and Judas—really got upset over their elder brother and His widespread acclaim. Knowing that a plot was rumored to be brewing among the Jewish leadership to dispose of Jesus, they came to Him just days before a major religious festival took place in Jerusalem.

Their advice? "You ought to go up to Jerusalem and show the crowds what you can do! If you're really who you say you are, that's where you belong. If you are overselling yourself and can't deliver, then stay away" (my contemporary paraphrase of John 7:3-4, but that was the essence of their harangue). Their cynicism was only thinly veiled; Jesus knew exactly what they meant. His public image wasn't on their minds. Their lives would have been simpler, in their view, with Him out of the picture.

Jesus sent them up to Jerusalem without Him and later went there alone, quietly and without fanfare. It was better for Him to spend the holiday alone than with these men who chose to distance themselves from Him and His purposes.

For some people, the most traumatic time of the year is the holiday season. I've talked to people who would rather scratch November and December off their calendar than go through the obligatory family gatherings. The reason is that their family is committed to their demise.

Too many people are chained to unhealthy relationships. They feel obligated to listen to and be swayed by people who want to destroy them. Jesus honored His family, but that didn't mean He had to agree with them.

An executive recently described to me his experience as the majority partner in a family business. During a particularly stressful time in the company's business cycle, he began to feel distance between himself and his father and brothers. He could not understand it, but the demands of declining revenues and operating losses kept him distracted from these relational issues.

One afternoon, his accountant called him at the office. My friend was aghast as he heard how his father and brothers had hired an investigator and an attorney to examine his activities. They had contacted the firm's CPA to obtain financial information in an effort to construct a case of malfeasance against him.

With nothing to hide, the CEO encouraged his accountant to cooperate with the effort, knowing there was no risk to him. After waiting a few weeks to let his emotions cool, he confronted his family members with what he had heard.

They admitted they were looking for evidence of surreptitious dealings that could explain the company's current woes. They simply did not believe his explanation of the facts. They grudgingly admitted they had been unable to discover even one element of dishonesty in his conduct. Even then they still said they didn't trust him.

The *coup de grace* came when the invoices arrived for the services of the investigator and attorney. The innocent CEO was asked to foot the bill for his own inquisition!

It's a fact that we don't choose the family into which we were born. Some of our friendships and associates come without our choice too. When those relationships impact us negatively, we need to adjust. It's not that we ignore them, but we don't have to let them govern our lives. The people I need to be with most are those who believe what I believe, not the people who shared an address with me before I had a choice in the matter.

Avoid the Stress of Unrealistic Expectations

I was driving home after dark and came to a stop at a traffic light. Across the street stood a familiar office building, and on the top floor, on the northeast corner, the lights still blazed. It happened that the tenth floor housed the firm led by a friend of mine named Sean.

From my car, I dialed Sean on his private line. He answered, and I asked, "What are you doing there at this hour?"

"I can't leave yet. I'm not finished," he replied weakly.

Now, I had known Sean for more than a decade. He's a "Type A" poster kid. Evenings, weekends and Sunday mornings, he's liable to be caught with his briefcase open. In all the years I've known him, he's never been "finished."

"Hey, listen, friend," I said. "If you stay there all night, will you be able to finish what you're working on?"

It took him longer to answer than it did for me to get a green light. Finally, he admitted that he wouldn't.

"Well, since you can't finish anyway, I'm giving you permission to go home. I'll call your wife to tell her to expect you. I'm going to keep going around the block until I see your lights go out." Sure enough, within a minute the lights went out and Sean was released from his self-imposed slavery to an unreasonable expectation.

Sean's behavior isn't terribly unusual. Most men and women I know who have made it to responsible career positions believe they should do twice what their priorities say they should. They act as if God had inspired the writing of their job descriptions, and they're willing to die trying to live up to the responsibilities described in that document.

Maybe it's time to reexamine your personal expectations of performance or those imposed on you by your superiors. Some people succumb to marching orders that should never have been given, and they never take the time to contest them.

....

Some people succumb to
marching orders that should never
have been given, and they never take
the time to contest them.

....

Jesus was definitely *not* stressed by unrealistic expectations. In the accounts from Scripture, have you noticed that

Jesus carried no smart phone on His belt, dictating His day-to-day—and minute-by-minute—activities? We see Him going from town to town, from village to village, teaching in the synagogues, preaching to the crowds, healing the sick. We're told that when He saw the crowds, He had compassion on them. He stopped, spent time with them and met them at their place of need.

But He didn't do it all. In the midst of a particularly demanding day, He told His disciples that the harvest was plentiful but the workers were few, and they should pray for God to send more workers (see Luke 10:2). In other words, they needed to help!

When we learn about God, we discover that He transcends time. One day for Him is like a thousand years, and a thousand years is like a day (see 2 Pet. 3:8). Now, I've spent some days at the office that seemed like a thousand years. But this is different. God stepped into time and spent 33 years facing the same time constraints we face. Jesus had approximately three years to fulfill His mission. There was more to do than one person could do. What would our culture tell Him? Work nights. Work weekends. Cancel your vacation. But never admit that there's more than you can handle. That's un-American!

Has anyone come to you and suggested that you go home when the sun goes down, or that you take a vacation? If so, you're fortunate. Most companies I know are willing to allow you to operate on the most unrealistic expectations. Jesus wasn't like that. He knew what He could do. When He reached His limit as a human, He said, "Hey, why don't you guys call headquarters and ask for reinforcements? There's more than we can do here."

If Jesus had limited capacity as a human being, doesn't that suggest that we're limited too? If He couldn't do it all, it's unlikely that you and I can do it all. But I know many people who live with a chain of unrealistic expectations firmly locked around their ankles. They're in slavery. They say they can't leave because there's more to do. Perhaps they don't need more time, they need more help.

If you're feeling bound to the office, if you feel you can't ever get it all done, you have permission to admit your limits. It's okay to shut off the lights, go home and spend time with your family. Take a break!

See Through the Attraction of Temporary Prosperity

Cheri and I had decided to spend a quiet New Year's Eve with our friends Ben and Sharon. After a great dinner, we spread out the Monopoly game to pass the time before midnight. With hours to play out the game to a win-lose conclusion, I quickly got into the spirit. This was Wall Street on the dining room table.

Our personality differences soon became apparent in the strategies we employed. Ben acquired a few properties he developed extensively while I employed a more diversi-fied strategy—utilities, transportation and a wide spread of residential real estate. Sharon was challenging my lead as we competed for control, while Cheri spent her money like a sailor on leave, blissfully enjoying the trip around the board.

As my wife ran low on funds, she happened upon the hotel-ridden Boardwalk controlled by "Trump," aka Ben. "I can't pay the rent," she sighed as Ben read the numbers from the back of the card.

Ben smiled and said, "That's okay! Pay me when you can."

Sharon and I exploded as if we were a duet: "If she can't come up with the dough, she's outta here!"

"That's the point of the game," I railed. "There are winners and losers. And she's a loser!"

As soon as the words escaped my mouth, I could see it was going to be a long drive home. I had committed a cardinal mistake: I forgot that what we were playing was just a game. I was so caught up in making deals that it became reality in my mind. I risked marital harmony in the holiday weekend just to load up my stack of play money.

Life's not really that different. Business is just a big Monopoly game, yet most of us treat it like it's the main event. The more I understand what Jesus taught, the more aware I am that one of these days God is going to come along, tap us on the shoulder and say, "The game's over." Then He's going to pick up the board, slide all of the pieces back into the box and call it quits . . .

....

Business is just a big Monopoly game, yet most of us treat it like it's the main event.

....

Jesus talked a lot about money. Have you ever thought about what money is for? Jesus says this is what it is for: "Use worldly wealth to gain friends for yourselves, so that when it is gone, you will be welcomed into eternal dwellings" (Luke 16:9).

"Now wait a minute!" you protest. "God is saying to use money to buy friends? I thought you were supposed to use money to buy stocks or cars or houses or income-producing property." No, Jesus said to use money to buy friends. Why? He says you can either use temporary money to buy temporary things, or you can use temporary money to buy eternal things. Is it better merely to trade on the Monopoly board, or to take Monopoly money and buy something of real value? Smart people use money in a way that will benefit them for a long period, not just a short time.

Alan and Katharine Barnhart are a remarkable couple who live in Memphis, Tennessee. Early in their lives together, they had honest conversations about their career options. They considered a future in foreign missions—deployed to countries hostile to the gospel, but Alan opted for the chance to take over his parents' business and reinvent it using a different worldview.

The Barnharts made what seemed then—and now—a radical commitment: They would build a business using the best practices, but they would build their lives using Jesus' model for best practice.

What's so different about that? For one thing, they set a limit on their income and their lifestyle—just like they would have done had they made "missions" their career path. They established what they believed was a reasonable income for a family with six children, retained the reasonable capital requirements for their construction services business . . . and would give the rest to the spread of the Kingdom around the world.

For more than two decades, God has allowed their business to expand at a rate of more than 25 percent per year. In the process, they have invested millions of their excess profits in people—just like Jesus suggested—and have "bought" friends for themselves who will someday welcome them into eternal dwellings.

The Pharisees heard Jesus tell this radical story about the use of money, and they sneered at Him. He had an answer for them, too. "You are the ones who justify yourselves in the eyes of men," he said, "but God knows your hearts. What is highly valued among men is detestable in God's sight" (Luke 16:15).

Now, that's a sobering thought: What is highly valued among men is detestable to God. He was specifically talking to people who love money. God says they had the wrong value system. His value system says to use temporary things (like money) for eternal purposes.

Jesus spent no time trying to accumulate temporary wealth. Do you know why? Simply put, why spend time chasing something that's temporary when you can spend the same time chasing the eternal? That makes sense to me. The problem is that I don't think about it often enough.

Mastering Your Life

1. Review the following and rate yourself from 1 to 10—with 10 being totally free and 1 meaning that you are totally in bondage:

   (a) Too often, I am bound to ineffective traditions.
   (b) Too often, I am distracted by unhealthy relationships.
   (c) Too often, I am stressed by unrealistic expectations.
   (d) Too often, I am enamored by temporary prosperity.

2. Pick the one with the lowest score. What is one thing you can do in this area to move toward greater freedom?

3. Commit yourself to implement your plan in this area within the next week.

COMMITMENT

A homebuilding company in my community enjoys a reputation for integrity and quality. While the principals in the company are Christian, they attract respect rather than scorn because of their philosophy and conduct. Their unusual status is due, in part, to an exercise they undertook when the company was founded.

Before they tackled their first commercial venture, the company founders huddled together to define their corporate values. What emerged were the "Fieldstone Values"—six statements of ethical foundation that have been the keystone of operations ever since. Every employee at the Fieldstone Company is instructed in these values. On every desk is a business card-sized summary of these values. Every employee also carries them in a pocket. At each Christmas party, awards are given to the employees who have demonstrated exemplary performance within each of the six values.

Fieldstone takes these essentials seriously. Workers are not disciplined for mistakes that cost the firm money. Rather, they are disciplined for decisions at odds with the company's values, even if the decision profited the corporation. To them, values are more important than income.

One of the partners in the company told me about a decision made by a middle manager that ended up costing the firm a significant sum of money. In most other companies, the manager would have been fired. It was the type of situation where a corporation's values are shown to be real or mere window dressing.

The partners reviewed the scenario in light of the company values, and it was determined that the manager's actions were in keeping with them. Though he cost the firm money through the option he chose, the only other choice available would have violated those values. Because he made a values-based decision, he was commended. Now there's a firm more interested in protecting its credibility than its capital.

In recent days, Wall Street has seen its public image move from exemplary to suspect because of the revelations of conduct that pitted value against values, with value—as measured in personal financial gain—winning. The Great Recession—whose beginning and ending points still remain points of contention—is really the consequence of our marketplace culture losing the values war.

It would be interesting to see a daily truth index included with the Dow Jones Industrial Average and other stock exchange quotes. For many, truth is no longer objective and absolute. It has become a drifting value that moves up or down based on the morals of the day. An increasing percentage of the population views truth as vacillating, unreal and nebulous. The standard is public image, not getting caught, and making as much money as possible.

....

For many, truth is no longer objective and absolute. It has become a drifting value that moves up or down based on the morals of the day.

....

But there are some people, like the partners at Fieldstone, who hold that values are more important than short-term profit, for they define who you are and your reputation. These people aren't necessarily unsuccessful. On the contrary, their success can often be attributed to their values. It's this commitment that defines life and gives it meaning.

Of what does this commitment consist? I submit that there are two essential elements: a set of basic core values and a willingness to defend those values when they are attacked.

Clarify the Core Values Worth Defending

It is popular to denounce people as dogmatic when they hold strong views. By knowing the issues that are absolute, however, we can determine when and how to defend our cause. Separating nonessential opinion from inviolate truth is the first step. If there are inarguable realities, dogmatism is called for and appropriate.

Henry Ward Beecher once said, "Whatever is only almost true is quite false, and among the most dangerous of errors because being so near truth, it is most likely to lead astray." Many people like to play horseshoes with the truth, saying that close is good enough. Dogmatic people are viewed with alarm, for they threaten the security of others.

Many people feel safe when they are free to redefine truth subjectively. When someone gets loose in the camp preaching the idea of moral absolutes, the person with a "whatever turns you on" credo gets unsettled. Dogmatic people can really be irritating with their message of invariable standards of right and wrong!

There are three classes of issues. The first level concerns things that are irrelevant. It doesn't matter that we disagree at this level. We may compare the color of our cars. You may say red is the best, and I will say silver. Now, while I may say your car is nice, I'll be thinking, *I'd never buy a car that color.* But it won't have anything to do with our relationship.

At level two are issues on which compromise is possible. If we're in business together and the decision is about building a fleet of cars, I might prefer efficient gas engines and you might want to go with electric. The decision isn't crucial to the direction of the company, so we decide to compromise: we buy eco-hybrids. There should be many areas where we are willing to give ground because foundational issues are not at stake.

It's at level three where we find the non-negotiables. These are those few issues about which we must be dogmatic. This is bedrock truth to be defended at all costs.

Jesus was a perfect example of someone who had clearly defined His core values. As we examine His life, we see there were many areas where He was willing to compromise. In fact, that was one reason He got into so much trouble with religious authorities, for He did not consider their traditions inviolable. Just what were His core values? We may be surprised at the things Jesus considered absolute.

The Purity of Religion

Shortly after Jesus began His public ministry, He visited Jerusalem. Passover, their most important Jewish festival, was about to begin. In the outer courtyard of the Temple, Jesus found a rowdy marketplace. Large amounts of money were being exchanged and sacrificial cattle, sheep and doves were being sold at inflated rates. It was a lot like the way Christmas has become commercialized in our own time, burying the significance of the birth of the Christ child.

How did Jesus respond? He made a whip and drove the merchandizers out of the Temple, along with their animals. "Get these out of here!" He shouted. "How dare you turn my Father's house into a market!" (see John 2:13-16.)

Today, we find many people turned off by Christianity because of the occasional revelation of corruption of some of high-visibility media preachers. These televangelists have used religion as a marketable item from which to draw a tremendous financial return. They've corrupted the purity that God intended.

Perhaps one reason Jesus got so upset with the market inside the Temple was that it stood in the Court of the Gentiles, where non-Jews were permitted. It was intended as a place where people from all over the world could come to find out about God. But instead of encountering God, they were separated from their money. Jesus considered that a defamation of God's character. (We'll look later at the way Jesus confronted this problem.)

The Necessity of Conversion

Shortly after the Temple confrontation, a man named Nicodemus came to see Jesus. Nicodemus was a highly regarded religious leader. If you lived in Israel and had any questions about religion, Nicodemus was the man to see. Religiously speaking, he was top dog.

But even Nicodemus recognized that Jesus had a supernatural authority. Jesus shocked him by saying, "No one can see the kingdom of God unless he is born again" (John 3:3). He meant that unless we are supernaturally transformed, we'll never be a part of God's plan. There must be a moment of conversion.

Perhaps you are like many people today who consider themselves Christians. They assume affiliation with God because of their connection to a recognized church or because they've been raised in a home by parents who held Christian beliefs. When asked about religion, most North Americans probably aren't going to say they're Muslim or Buddhist, Scientologist or Sikh. So, of course, they're Christian.

Jesus disputed all of that. He said we are not Christians because of upbringing or affiliation. If we are Christians, it is because we have made a conscious decision to surrender to the Spirit of God. Jesus was dogmatic about that. Unless you buy into this bedrock truth, you are separated from Him.

The Exclusivity of Christianity

Jesus made some audacious statements in His life. For instance, He said, "I am the way and the truth and the life. No one comes to [God] the Father except through me" (John 14:6). Jesus didn't say He was "a" way or "a" truth or "a" life. He used the definite article. He was not one option among many, but the only way to reach God.

If you're involved in product distribution, you know how valuable a territory is when you own exclusive rights to it. How valuable would those rights be if, after you've paid a hefty fee to represent that product or service, you discover that many others have the same right to provide the same product to the same customers? An exclusive right means that in your market area no other source exists to obtain your product. People have to come directly to you or they can't obtain the product.

Jesus said He had an exclusive right to represent God on earth. Try to call God the Father direct, and He will direct all calls back through Jesus. There are a lot of people trying to figure out a way to make room for anyone who worships the great cosmos in the sky—as long as that person is sincere: "You don't need Jesus, you don't need the cross; there are other ways to heaven." Not according to Jesus! He says He's the only authorized distributor, and if you don't go through Him, you don't get the product. It's that simple.

You want to be called dogmatic? Tell people that Christianity provides the only way to get to heaven. They'll say you are dogmatic, and they'll be right. But if Jesus spoke the truth, we can't afford not to make this a core value.

The Window of Opportunity

Finally, Jesus was intensely dogmatic about our window of opportunity. He said, "You are from below; I am from above. You are of this world; I am not of this world. I told you that you would die in your sins; if you do not believe that I am the one I claim to be, you will indeed die in your sins" (John 8:23-24).

That's pretty narrow, isn't it? A lot of people believe in the second chance. They somehow think that after they die, God will take them to a little waiting room and say, "This is your last chance, buddy." That's not what Jesus said. He spoke of a window of opportunity, and if you miss it, it's gone forever.

Rob Bell was a pastor in Michigan with an international podcast following. He was a new voice in the Christian camp and he found many eager listeners who relied on his insights as credible and believable.

Then he wrote a book that was more speculative than certain. In his book *Love Wins*, he imagined a God who would offer do-overs—after death—for people who didn't get the faith-in-Jesus-during-this-life thing quite right.

He is in sync with a modern culture more comfortable with ambiguity, but he is at odds with a Founder—the Lord Jesus—who drew a line in the sand with a countdown clock called "life," within which each of us will make an eternal, binding decision.

We're all familiar with this concept in day-to-day life. If you want to take advantage of certain tax breaks, you have to act before December 31. If you want to respond to a business proposition, you have to act according to a time frame; the opportunity won't last forever. If you want to buy your significant other a Christmas or Valentine's gift, you have to act before December 25 or February 14.

Concerning the biggest deal we will ever face in life, Jesus said there is a window of opportunity. The one difference between this one and the others is that for the IRS or a holiday gift there is a countdown: we know exactly when it will happen. But we don't know when life will end. It could be 50 years from now, or it could be tomorrow.

Jesus was dogmatic about this. He called this dogmatism *truth*. Some people will find themselves eternally in a place they never planned to be because they didn't understand that one day the window would close and their chance would pass. Their opportunity to say yes to Jesus and to what He wanted to be in their lives would be gone forever.

The apostle Paul claimed that the gospel was so simple that those who trust only in their own wisdom would tend to dismiss it as foolish (see 1 Cor. 1:18-31). "Trust Jesus

Christ and what He did for us 2,000 years ago, surrender our lives to Him and believe that this will change our eternal destiny? That's too easy!" That's right, it is. But that's the gospel. It's our choice to do something about it.

Now, it's not enough merely to hold some fundamental convictions. LifeMastery requires that we defend those values when they are under attack. Jesus, the perfect man, also showed us how to do that.

Defend Basic Core Values When They Are Attacked

If a vote were taken pitting harmony against conflict, harmony would win hands down. It is for that reason that confrontation is often devalued. When harmony is held in highest esteem, however, the potential for serious error multiplies. If we value truth, we will face confrontation.

Jesus wasn't afraid of confrontation. Some of the most dramatic scenes in the Bible are those where Jesus debated the religious and political leaders of His day. When religious leaders questioned why He ate with "undesirables" like tax collectors, He could have ignored them. But He confronted them, saying, "It is not the healthy who need a doctor, but the sick. . . . I have not come to call the righteous, but sinners" (Matt. 9:12-13).

When Jesus was challenged about His disciples' failure to follow all the religious traditions of the day, Jesus called His accusers hypocrites: "You have let go of the commands of God and are holding on to the traditions of men" (Mark 7:8).

On another occasion, His disciples argued about who was the greatest. Jesus confronted them and used the occasion to explain that whoever wanted to be first had to be last, and servant of all (see Mark 9:33-37).

Some people claim that we do the same thing today with assertiveness training. Closer examination reveals, however, that much of this training is designed simply to protect your rights and to make sure your position doesn't get challenged, damaged or defamed. In other words, you learn how to stand up for what you have coming so no one can take it away from you.

That is not what we mean by confrontation, as practiced by Jesus. Confrontation deals not with the protection of your rights, but with the protection of your *values*. There is a major difference between the two. Most often, I need to let God fight the battle of my personal rights. When my rights are challenged, God says I can hand over my defense to Him; He will see to it that I'm protected. It is true that in the short term, I may find myself facing "third down and forty yards to go" just to get back to the line of scrimmage, but God says He'll take care of me.

Confrontation deals not with the protection of your rights, but with the protection of your *values*.

On the other hand, God encourages us to confront whenever our values are challenged. G. K. Chesterton once said, "I believe in getting into hot water; I think it keeps you clean." Some of us try to stay out of hot water at all costs. But there is danger in that. Our society lacks definition and intensity with regard to values because it doesn't like hot water. Hot water often means confrontation, and we try to avoid that. The theory goes like this: If you don't believe anything very deeply, you will never run into problems with people of opposing viewpoints. The more flexible we are with our values, the less likely we are to face confrontation.

I read recently about an Ivy League university that was given a $31 million grant to develop a business ethics program. The school is careful to make sure it doesn't suggest what those values should be; it simply teaches students how wonderful it is to have them. This university is spending $31 million to teach the value of values.

I suppose that's better than nothing; but to suggest that there are no absolute values endangers society. Frankly, I'm glad that the American Revolution occurred 200 years ago, when people valued freedom. I'm not sure that today a majority would decide to cut the strings to Great Britain. I don't think we hold values deeply enough to want to protect them and to confront those who challenge them.

I believe that by protecting the values that define your life you will illuminate your world. Frankly, if there is nothing in your life worth dying for there is nothing in your life worth living for. You are left with a lackluster existence that has purposelessness written all over it.

In my experience, people long for something or someone they can believe in. They want it so badly in fact, that they are capable of allying with losing teams in their rush to connect with something worth living for.

Alexander Hamilton said, "I'm sure that most of us looking back would admit that whatever we've achieved in character we've achieved through conflict." People who have become benchmarks of character, who have demonstrated the greatest personal achievement and progress, are people who have engaged in conflict when appropriate. They confronted the challenge to their fundamental values.

Some years ago, in Washington, D.C., a drama was played out through the courts, the penal system and the

Congress. A woman refused to deliver her daughter to the family court, accepting instead a contempt charge that put her in jail for more than two years. The reason? She is convinced that her former husband has a history of child sexual abuse and is capable of abusing his own child. The judge did not agree, and the principled mother demonstrated the depth of her resolve as she sat behind bars. Her fundamental commitment to her daughter was put to the test.

The greatest example of this courage to confront is Jesus of Nazareth. Let's return again to the case we examined earlier, where Jesus cleared out the moneychangers from the Temple. Actually, He did this twice. His gentle demeanor throughout His three-year public ministry was bracketed by two violent events. As we examine the historical records, we can find insight on three points: when it is appropriate to publicly react, how to defend your values, and why such a defense is necessary.

When a Defense Is Called for

The first reason for confronting faulty positions is to let the other side know you're there. A few years back, there was a great deal of talk about the "silent majority"—a large percentage of the populace that disagreed with societal trends but remained mute because it didn't want to wade into the fray. Far from being a defense, this strategy is a passionless default of personal beliefs. It is this strategy that allows for an immoral minority to prevail over a superior (but apathetic) force.

The first cleansing of the Temple was Jesus' first major public event. The previous events in his life occurred in isolated areas or in front of small crowds. The first thing Jesus did upon arriving in Jerusalem was to visit the Temple. Now, remember, there was no surprise here for Jesus. As

God, He fully knew what was happening in the outer courtyard. The commercialization and desecration of the holy sanctuary had been a fact of life for years. The all-knowing Son of God walked into that situation with His eyes open and acted with forethought and resolve.

Jesus moved decisively to communicate a message. He was in town! He was a person to be reckoned with. He stood opposed to the goings-on. He was on the side of right. He did not clean house in His own name, but as an agent of His Father: "Take these things away! Do not make My Father's house a house of merchandise" (John 2:16, *NKJV*).

Immediately afterward, He became the target of hostile questions from the Jewish leaders. He captured their attention and opened the dialogue that would continue in the public arena for the next three years. So the first reason for a defense is to let the other side know you're there.

A second good reason for undertaking a defense of your values is that it may be necessary to establish an environment for pursuing your mission. Suppose, for instance, that you are a schoolteacher in a public high school, and your mission statement calls you to impart your faith in Jesus Christ to teenagers. In respect to your professional duties, you don't use your classroom to give your testimony. But you serve as an involved faculty sponsor for a student-initiated and student-led Christian club that meets on campus. In that setting, you are able to respond to interested students about your beliefs.

A parent whose child has never attended one of your meetings confronts the school administration with a demand to deny the use of classroom space to the club during non-school hours, even though it meets all of the tests for sanctioned clubs imposed on any other group. The demand is based on the reasoning that such a club implies state establishment of religion and thus is unconstitutional. Should you, as a faculty member, put yourself in jeopardy by standing up for the club? It might be necessary to fulfill your mission.

Jesus found Himself in such a position after three years of ministry. He landed back in Jerusalem during the Passover, and again He set His sights on the Temple. It was like an instant replay. I'm sure some of the money merchants sighed under their breath, "Here we go again!" as Jesus moved angrily through the ranks, causing pandemonium and chasing them out of the courtyard.

Jesus had been in and out of Jerusalem during those three years of ministry. Yet, He had not moved against these corrupters during those visits. Why, after all this time, would He again challenge their improper activities in the Temple courts?

It certainly wasn't because He thought He could fix the problem. In a few days, He would be crucified. Seven weeks later, He would return to heaven, His mission fulfilled. But the Temple would be back to its former clutter and confusion. His cleansing was but a temporary respite from the trend toward unholiness.

So why was the Sunday of His last week spent sweeping out the dirt in the House of God? He was clearing the platform for His final presentation. During the next four days, He presented divine truth in this Temple courtyard. Some of His most significant teaching occurred during this time, and we read that while the religious leaders were plotting to kill Him, the crowd flocked to hear His teaching. Clearing the area provided the proper environment for pursuing His mission. Completing the work God had given Him to do was primary. Jesus would do whatever was necessary to assure the satisfactory completion of that agenda.

How to Mount a Defense

This example might sound like a call for religious radicalism. Does this mean we are supposed to become Christian Rambos? Does the driven believer violate biblical principles and the laws of the land in pursuit of a godly objective? Some would think so.

Jesus, however, makes a great case for conscientious activism conducted with deliberate control. In every account of the Temple cleansings, the record is the same: Jesus interrupted the status quo without abandoning His integrity. He drove the people out but never abused them. He put them out of the Temple but not into the hospital. In His drive to respect God's property, He also respected their property. He wasn't against them; He was against what they were doing.

There is something unique about His approach, because His conduct didn't hinder His reception with the onlookers. Luke says that He cleaned out the merchandisers and then began to teach, reporting that the people all "hung on his words" (Luke 19:48). That's the great test: You know you've responded incorrectly to the opposition when, as a result of your actions, you lose credibility rather than win it.

> You know you've responded
> incorrectly to the opposition when,
> as a result of your actions, you lose
> credibility rather than win it.

One Watergate participant whose prominence skyrocketed after the Nixon era was the late Chuck Colson. Then Special Counsel to the President, Colson became a Christian just before serving time for his part in the Watergate scandal.

After his release, he founded Prison Fellowship, a ministry to prisoners around the world, and he became an outspoken advocate for penal reform in America and abroad. From that platform, Colson spent the rest of his life as a spokesman for faith and freedom, and he was an eloquent defender of the values modeled by the Lord Jesus.

With the eloquence of a politician and the credibility of a statesman, Colson boldly confronted the status quo as he appealed for a new approach to the growing prison populace. He went head-to-head with the custodians of conventional wisdom in government as he called for redemptive treatment for all.

Though at odds with his adversaries on this issue, he won the respect of politicians and bureaucrats through his integrity and character. Though they may not have agreed with his position, they admired his commitment to the cause. He successfully gained credibility even when he hadn't gained adherents. He died as a respected patriot and, even more, a modern-day apostle for the Christian movement.

Why We Need to Defend the Truth

The history of Christianity has been written around the life stories of men and women who could not be silenced. They were sure of what they believed, and they were unstoppable in its proclamation.

Attacks on truth are not new. During the first century, church leader Jude urged Christians to "contend for the faith that was once for all entrusted to the saints" (Jude 1:3). The earliest protagonists varied in personality and temperament, but they agreed on strategy. Peter, the rough and tough fisherman, said he could not "help speaking what we have seen and heard" (Acts 4:20). Paul, the educated and erudite spokesman for the faith, found himself

138   BOB SHANK

"reasoning daily" (Acts 19:9, *NKJV*) in settings as divergent as a hilltop meeting of Athenian philosophers and a synagogue of devout Jews in Asia.

Centuries later, in 1517, Martin Luther put his life on the line when he nailed his 95 theses to the door of a church in Wittenberg, Germany, and paved the way for the Protestant Reformation. In the twentieth century, Martin Luther King Jr., took his defense of racial equality to the point of death, and Watchman Nee held fast to the truth of the gospel despite tortures and, eventually, martyrdom in a Chinese prison. The defenders of truth make up a mighty fraternity throughout history.

Mastering Your Life

Is it better to defend truth or tolerate a lie? I have never seen a statue erected to the memory of heroic tolerance. But I have seen them established to memorialize a love for truth, expressed to the point of great personal sacrifice.

Confrontation isn't necessary until you hold some values worth defending. One reason we acquiesce rather than confront is that we honor harmony over fuzzy values. In the space below, make a list of your five most important values. Next to this list, note the last time someone challenged those values. What did you do? Did you confront the attack on your basic values? If so, did you sense an inward satisfaction, or frustration in the encounter?

1. _____
2. _____
3. _____
4. _____
5. _____

] 10 [

AVAILABILITY

While it's easy to dismiss mission-driven people as insensitive, no one ever did that with Jesus. He was deliberate about where He was going and what He was doing, but He also allowed Himself to be detoured by needy people. Some men and women are so mission-oriented that they forget people. Others are so people-oriented that they forget mission. Jesus avoided both errors.

How can we strike a balance? We do so through the practice of availability.

It's appropriate to consider this now after concentrating on such things as mission and control. Without balance, we can find ourselves growing depersonalized. The control-driven, mission-minded lifestyle must be complemented by the recognition that there are individuals with legitimate claims on our time and resources. Our objective is not to become so driven and intense that we become blind to these people, for people define our life.

How do we balance these conflicting principles? We do it by establishing an agenda and using that agenda instead of serving a schedule. People who use an agenda will have time for those who require their attention even though they have no appointment. Some of the most important meetings in your day are not depicted in your digital calendar.

I was knee-deep in deadlines one Friday and essentially checked-out so far as the people on my staff were concerned. They were to consider me invisible to any demands that day; I told them that I could not be disturbed.

Despite my strategic firewall, my secretary rang through to my office to tell me I had an urgent call. She gave me the name of the woman who was calling, and I didn't know her. I took the call anyway.

She sounded desperate and emotionally stretched. "No, you don't know me, but you would recognize my husband. We've really got to see you. Things are at a crisis point. We'll come anywhere. Just tell us what we have to do."

I looked at my schedule that was lined out for the day. I looked at my desk piled high with past-due projects. I looked at my watch. The day was escaping while I was talking on the phone.

My schedule said no, but my agenda said *yes!* My agenda is people, not projects. My prime targets are hurting people with no other connections. I had 10 reasons why I wasn't free, but none of them held up when confronted by someone who fit the profile for my life agenda.

This couple came to my office within the hour and stayed for three more. At the end of that time, their marriage took a turn for the better after two years of marital decline punctuated by dramatic pitfalls and hurtful revelations. It was the best possible use of my day. Had I known about it in advance, I would have scheduled the meeting. Had I stuck to my schedule, I would have missed it.

What is the difference between agenda and schedule? An agenda is a profile of things to be done. A schedule is a list of things to be done in a certain time frame.

It's the element of time that confuses us. We are so driven by the clock that the issues of timing and order become paramount; in fact, protecting our precious time is sometimes more important than the things that really need to be done.

> We are so driven by the clock that the issues of timing and order become paramount; in fact, protecting our precious time is sometimes more important than the things that really need to be done.

When I look at the life of Jesus, I am impressed that although He lived only 33 years and spent only three-and-a-half years in public ministry, at the time of His death He could say, "It is finished." He had completed the work He came to do. How could that be? The answer is found in the way He used an agenda rather than serving a schedule. By living this way, He found time for those who required His attention, even though they came to Him without an appointment. The same principle can work for us.

Let's look at three factors governing Jesus' availability, and how those factors apply to us today.

Take Time to Formalize Your Agenda

There is an intriguing example that comes out of the last century's political history. One of the most significant figures of the Reagan presidency may be a man who occupied a position that's normally out of the public eye. How many surgeon generals can you name? Dr. C. Everett Koop took an often obscure position and distinguished it.

What was it that burned his memory into the American consciousness? It was not primarily his military uniform or his odd gray beard, but rather his bold and controversial positions regarding smoking, AIDS, sex education, abortion and other public health issues. Ironically, it was a period of personal humiliation that ultimately led to his success.

When Dr. Koop was nominated for surgeon general, he had to go through a laborious confirmation process by the Senate. His strong views led to vehement opposition from groups such as Planned Parenthood and the National Organization for Women. What was expected to be a quick confirmation turned into a nine-month battle.

For years, Dr. Koop had worked long hours as a world-renowned pediatric surgeon. Now, as he waited for Congress to complete its hearings about his nomination, he had nothing to do. It was a frustrating situation for a man with enormous energy. Every day, he went to a large but empty office and found nothing on his appointment calendar. What could he do with that time?

He found that this interlude was a wonderful gift—a time to think about the difference he could make as surgeon general. He developed plans for helping the cause of handicapped children, the elderly, battered women and children and others in need. "During that nine months I developed a detailed agenda, something no surgeon general has ever had before," he said. "In the end, that period of acute frustration made possible every single thing I was able to accomplish in office. Now that's the sovereignty of God at work!"[1]

As a result of formalizing his agenda, Dr. Koop was not content to speak only when spoken to. He was unwilling to quiet the waters at all costs. He did not plan to speak softly and carry a big stick. The corporate and financial interests that were threatened by his ethically motivated pronouncements against unhealthful products could not silence him.

As trustee of the national health, he set his agenda and pursued it tirelessly. He left office having made a mark on his world like no person in that position before him. He was proactive, not reactive. He set the cadence to which he marched.

That's what Jesus did. Soon after He began His public career at the age of 30, Jesus returned home and attended the local synagogue on what was, for most people, *just another Sabbath*. There He was asked to be guest speaker. They handed Him one of the sacred scrolls. He opened it and read the following from the prophet Isaiah:

> The Spirit of the Lord is on me, because he has anointed me to preach good news to the poor. He has sent me to proclaim freedom for the prisoners and recovery of sight for the blind, to release the oppressed, to proclaim the year of the Lord's favor" (Luke 4:18-19; see Isa. 61:1-2).

When He finished reading, Jesus announced to the congregation, "Today this scripture is fulfilled in your hearing" (Luke 4:21). Jesus wanted His audience to understand that this was no random selection from the Bible. It was written centuries earlier to spell out His agenda . . . and it gave the overview of His historic mission.

That was His agenda. So the natural question arises, "How does agenda vary from purpose?" Purpose is the rock-solid definition of direction in your life. Once you've determined why you're here, your purpose doesn't change. An agenda is the means by which, *for a period of time,* your purpose or mission is served. It is a list of things that have to be done to advance your mission.

Without an agenda, you quickly slip into a response mode. You arrive at the office every day and your activities are determined by your telephone calls and walk-ins. Your email in-box can divert your direction for the morning before your latte turns cold. You do what seems appropriate in response to life. You become reactive instead of taking initiative.

I wager that people who are significant are rarely known as first responders. It is people with initiative who go places and get things done. They have an agenda for life and work each day at implementing it. But having an agenda is just the first step. You need to get more specific for it to work.

Develop a Strategy to Pursue Your Agenda

Soon after Jesus announced His agenda, He found Himself swamped with people in Capernaum. He taught them, cast out demons and healed the sick. He was doing what He said He would do. And He did it well enough that people wanted to invade His life. He was up late but still managed to rise early the next morning and slip away to a lonely place. People went looking for Him. They didn't want Him to leave; they wanted Him to preach some more, to continue what He had started.

But Jesus said, "I must preach the good news of the kingdom of God to the other towns also, because that is why I was sent" (Luke 4:43). The people of Capernaum said their strategy was to keep Jesus for themselves. They wanted Him to perform His agenda there and only there. But Jesus rejected that idea. He said, "I'm taking my agenda all over. That's why I came." With His strategy so clear, He wasn't going to be distracted from it.

I try to use my vacation each year to do more than work on a tan. One thing I do is read the latest installment in my autobiography. Whether you know it or not, you're writing an autobiography. You complete two chapters each year, both indisputably accurate. The journals that archive your life so irrefutably are your datebook and your checkbook. Show me those two records and I'll tell you your priorities, purpose and agenda.

....

The journals that archive your
life so irrefutably are your datebook
and your checkbook.

....

A few years ago, I reviewed my last 12 months through the window of my schedule and was taken aback. My life showed a frightening trend. I was participating in multiple outside agendas at the expense of my own.

It didn't happen because I lacked an agenda. If you asked me, I could have rattled off my mission statement, my vision, my agenda and my strategy, and you would have walked away impressed. Trouble was, my expression of that agenda was slipping, and nothing would change unless I did something about it.

Although I was in the last week of preparation for a much-needed three-week family vacation, I found myself parked in a restaurant booth, awaiting the arrival of a man I had never met. He had convinced me, through my assistant, that he really needed an hour of my day; and as I waited, I couldn't fathom how he had managed that.

Until he came, I reviewed the prior month. My attention focused on the meals I had spent with people who had chased me—people selling something, people looking for career positions, people with no clear agenda who came recommended by some mutual acquaintance. People who had taken hour upon hour of my time with no benefit ultimately gained for anyone.

I thought also about the guys I wanted to influence, but for whom I hadn't made time. These were the leaders who didn't normally chase me for time but were ready when I had it available. No doubt their patience wore thin as I sat waiting for yet another "blind date" lunch appointment.

It was another dud, but I gained from that lunch greatly. I flew back into my office afterward and sat down across the desk from my assistant. I handed her a list of 50 men with whom I wanted to spend time, and I asked her to call them while I was on vacation. When I returned, I had 50 appointments scheduled in the coming weeks.

The best solution to my problem was to take control. I wouldn't have time to meet with the timewasters, because I would already be committed to the people I really needed to be with, based on my purposeful agenda.

What followed was an amazingly productive quarter. It was such a good move that I committed to myself to do it again!

Every hour in your day, every meeting you're in, every phone call you take either advances your agenda or someone else's. I try to measure how much of my time I am deliberately directing, and how much is falling prey to the demands of others. In some of my past years, someone else was beating the drum, and I was marching.

That day, I spent time rethinking my strategies for advancing my agenda. I asked myself what I needed to do; with whom I needed to spend time; and how much I needed to be "unavailable." Then I carved those items into my future time frames.

Some relief has come since doing that exercise. But it remains a daily challenge to remain the director of my own God-honoring strategy rather than to become a pawn in some other person's plan for my life.

Next, we're ready to deal with a most important concept. It has to do with interruptions, those unplanned and unscheduled moments that seem to throw you off course. They may not be what they first appear.

Allow Your Agenda to Interrupt Your Schedule

Jesus allowed His agenda to supersede His schedule. Sometimes, when He had other things planned, He allowed people to interrupt. I'm convinced that most of us are willing to be available to the right people. They have instant access. But others don't get through your assistant. If they asked for an appointment, you would do anything necessary to dodge them.

And that may be okay. Most of us, however, probably do not make those decisions from the right value system. I know that by looking at Jesus. With Him, the people who got through were the least likely ones. They were the ones our systems would probably screen. Let's look at several cases.

One time, Jesus was leaving the city of Jericho accompanied by His disciples and a large crowd. A blind man sat on the roadside, begging. When he heard that Jesus was passing by, he began to shout, "Jesus, Son of David, have mercy on me!" Many in the crowd rebuked the man and told him to be quiet. After all, he was an undesirable, a derelict. Useless. Why bother the Master?

But Jesus stopped and ordered the crowd to call him. When they called the blind man, he jumped to his feet and came to Jesus.

"What do you want me to do for you?" Jesus asked him.

"Rabbi, I want to see," the man replied.

"Then you have it!" Jesus answered. Immediately the man received his sight. While the crowd despised this man, Jesus took time for him and met his need (see Luke 18:35-43).

On another occasion, Jesus was on His way to the home of a man named Jairus, whose daughter lay dying (see Luke 9). Jairus was a ruler of the synagogue, a position of great influence. Time was of the essence, for the girl couldn't last much longer. Unfortunately, a traffic jam developed on the road. The bumper-to-bumper crowd nearly crushed Jesus.

In the midst of this mob stood a woman who for 12 years had suffered from hemorrhaging. No doctor had been able to heal her. In desperation, she touched the edge of Jesus' cloak; instantly she was healed.

Jesus could have kept right on going; after all, He was in a hurry, and the woman no doubt would have preferred anonymity. It's hard to imagine that Jesus even noticed this particular touch in the jostling crowd, anyway. But He stopped and asked, "Who touched me?" The woman was scared. But when she saw that Jesus wouldn't leave until she identified herself, she came trembling and fell at His feet to explain why she had touched Him and how she had been instantly healed.

It's important to understand the significance of this encounter. Her condition made her an outcast; the possibility of infecting others meant she could have no contact with society. In the Jewish vernacular, she was considered "unclean."

And here is Jesus, rushing to His most important meeting of the day, stopping to talk to one of the most undesirable people of that time. He's instantly available to a woman who has no entrée to the rest of society. The least likely person has His full attention, and He solves her problem.

The situation soon becomes even more complicated. While Jesus is delayed, Jairus's daughter dies, and his servants arrive to relay the news: it won't be necessary to trouble Jesus any further. But Jesus isn't ignoring the need of Jairus. Just as He met the need of this poor woman, He will meet the need of the synagogue ruler. He continues on to the ruler's home and raises the little girl from the dead.

A third example of Jesus' availability came in His encounter with a traitorous taxman (see Luke 19:1-10). (Some may think those terms are synonymous and, hence, redundant!) Jesus was passing through Jericho again. In that city lived a man named Zacchaeus, a chief tax collector and a wealthy man. Because he was short, he couldn't see Jesus through the crowd, so he ran ahead and climbed a tree. When Jesus reached that spot, He looked up at Zacchaeus and said, "Come down immediately. I must stay at your house today."

Tax collection in that day was like McDonald's is today: they were franchised. You could bid for a tax district to the Roman government and agree to pay them a certain per-capita rate. Anything you collected over and above that, you could keep. Not a bad way to get rich, you say? True; but for a Jew, it also meant being ostracized by your community. Zacchaeus's own people considered him a traitor. Why would anyone want to be seen with this man?

Well, there was one who did: Jesus. He interrupted His trip through town to eat dinner with Zacchaeus. When no one else would talk to this man, Jesus did. As a result, Zacchaeus's life was changed. He promised to pay back all those he'd cheated and give half of all he owned to the poor. Jesus said, "Today salvation has come to this house."

There is a stark contrast between the questions, "Where are you supposed to be?" and "What are you trying to accomplish?" Sometimes we can focus too much on the first and not at all on the second.

Years ago, Dr. Billy Graham was engaged in a series of meetings in the Northeast. He was having a significant impact on thousands of people. The leaders and churches involved in hosting the meetings implored Dr. Graham to extend his time with them to take advantage of what God was doing in their midst.

Graham's schedule did not allow him to say yes to their request. A series of crusade meetings had been planned in Canada and were scheduled to begin just as the Northeast meetings were reaching their zenith. He left the certain moving of God's Spirit in the Northeast for the possibility of the Spirit's movement at meetings not yet begun.

Dr. Graham later reported that this was one of the most obvious mistakes of his career. His schedule was deemed more important than his agenda. God never arrived at the Canadian meetings in the way He had been apparent in the northeastern United States. The evangelist had kept his appointments at the expense of his mission.

Mastering Your Life

There are times when interrupting a man-made schedule is the right thing to do in view of a God-ordained agenda.

Your schedule is capable of disabling your agenda and destroying your effectiveness. Take a few minutes to list five things that warrant top billing on your agenda:

1. _____
2. _____
3. _____
4. _____
5. _____

After making this list, find a spot in your personal journal or digital calendar to archive these as a reminder. When you are faced with an opportunity to serve that agenda this week, do it, even if you lose ground in your schedule.

(Note: This applies to the portion of your schedule that is within your control; everyone has varying degrees of binding commitment to something outside their control. Focus on the aspects on which you call the shots.)

Note
1. Philip D. Yancey, "The Embattled Career of Dr. Koop," *Christianity Today*, October 20, 1989, p. 18

Focus

You've set your agenda. But now the intrusions arrive via text, email, phone call, snail mail and walk-ins. Hard as you try, you can't seem to stop these distractions from draining your energy. You're not as effective as you should be.

Some people think this is a *good* strategy. "Spread the risk," they say. "You never know what might work, so diversify." That may be a good financial investment strategy, but it's a disaster for personal success. To really make your energy count the most, you have to focus that energy on your mission.

In 1980, a repeat DWI offender killed a 13-year-old California girl in a car accident. Her mother, enraged at the leniency of the laws and judicial system toward drunk-driving cases, directed her energies toward changing society's position on drinking and driving.

In the next 10 years, Candace "Candy" Lightner mobilized America under the Mothers Against Drunk Driving (MADD) banner. Now more than 1.1 million supporters strong, they continue their march toward putting a final end to tragedies caused by alcohol-and-drug-impaired driving. This group's groundswell of passionate activity has resulted in a remarkably high name recognition among American adults. Annual deaths from drinking and driving have fallen because of their efforts, and hundreds of local chapters nationwide have provided effective lobbying to shape the legislative response to this problem. Educational programs aimed at prevention are now a major thrust of MADD's multipronged initiative. Truly, Lightner's focus on a tragic issue has helped change her world.

I maintain that Candy Lightner achieved her impact through her ability to focus. By narrowing her target and her objective, she succeeded in a critical area of life. So can you. Doesn't that have more appeal than sitting in your recliner and mailing in your monthly dues to the Flabby Fraternity of the Mediocre?

It's been said that no horse goes anywhere until he's harnessed; no steam drives anything until it's confined; no river generates any electricity until its channeled. Likewise, no life ever grows great until it is focused, dedicated and disciplined.

....

No life ever grows great until it is focused,
dedicated and disciplined.

....

Many men and women fail to leave a legacy of effective influence because they do not concentrate their energies and talents into a specific area. On the other hand, the greatest figures of history all knew how to focus. Having defined their purpose, they gave themselves fully to the enterprise.

Consider how this was true in the life of Jesus Christ. His three-and-a-half years of public ministry were highly focused, and the way He fixed His attention gives us insight into how we can focus.

Determine the Identity of Your Natural Market

First, notice that Jesus focused on a specific audience. He wasn't out to talk to the whole world. On one occasion, when he visited the region of Tyre and Sidon, a Canaanite woman came to him. Her daughter was suffering terribly from demon possession, and she begged Jesus for help.

Now, Jesus did help her—He demonstrated the balance between focus and availability—but before He did, he made this statement: "I was sent only to the lost sheep of Israel" (Matt. 15:24). Jesus made an exception in this case, but He wasn't going to be diverted from proclaiming His message to the Jews.

Did that mean He didn't have compassion for non-Jewish people? Not at all. But His intent was to focus on one group and to train a few people within that group. Later, after He returned to heaven, His followers would take His message to the world.

Jesus also focused within His target group. Early in His ministry, He befriended a tax collector named Matthew. Matthew was so thrilled that he invited all of his tax collector friends to his house to meet Jesus. This deeply offended the religious types, who complained to those who followed Jesus around.

Jesus didn't ignore their complaint. He answered, "It is not the healthy who need a doctor, but the sick. I have not come to call the righteous, but sinners" (Mark 2:17). In other words, Jesus identified two kinds of folk within His broad target market: those who didn't believe they had any needs, and those who didn't have any doubt that they did. Jesus said, "I've only got three-and-a-half years to work the territory. I'm not going to waste my time trying to convince people who think they've got it all together. I'm going to the people who know they need what I've got."

Since my days in business gave way to my life in ministry, I have always recognized that my personal focus was directed toward influencers. Some would just call them leaders, but my definition is far more specific than is suggested by a position statement on a business card. Some people have lofty titles but limited influence. Others lack official status but exercise significant influence over other people. In a digital age—with the rise of social networking and global connectivity—leadership has been redefined.

Within that influential minority are generational subgroupings. My age cohort—the now-aging Baby Boomers— seemed to lead the way regarding generational distinction.

Born in the U.S. between the years 1946 and 1964, we were raised on Hostess Cupcakes and Ozzie and Harriet. We watched the Rose Parade and the Viet Nam War from our living rooms in living color. We got more schooling, better jobs and higher salaries than the generation before us.

After we got comfortable with being uncomfortable with Baby Boomers, the Yuppies came along, then Generation X, then Gen Y, then the Millennials . . . all with their nuanced peculiarities germane to their coming-of-age peers.

My native tongue is Influencer, with a Boomer twang. Over the last three decades, I've had to learn the generational dialects that have allowed me to broaden my target market beyond just my Boomer peers to all Influencers, but born under different cultural administrations.

Many years ago, a friend invited me to speak at a New Year's weekend retreat for high schoolers (they would grow into Gen Xers, but they didn't know it yet!). My friend had heard me speak for events like that for adult peers and thought I'd do a great job with these kids.

Boy, was he wrong! There were 200 of them, and one of me. I couldn't connect with them for anything. Nothing worked. My silver tongue turned to tin. My humor came up moronic. The things that excited my Boomer crowds drove these teens up the wall. I was out of my element. I didn't speak a language they could understand.

Another time, I spent a week 2,000 miles from home speaking to a group of senior citizens from the agricultural communities of the heartland. Later dubbed The Greatest Generation, they were wonderful people, but I didn't know the first thing about their world. I could have used a translator. That week was the longest week of my life. I was convinced again that my primary market was very narrow and that I ignored it at my own peril.

If you are most effective with a particular, identifiable type or group of people, doesn't it make sense to spend the majority of your time with them? I know folks who make up their minds to talk to whomever calls. I'm convinced that if your schedule is filled primarily with people who have asked to see you, you're probably unfocused and ineffective.

Now, Jesus certainly was available to those occasional people who came to Him even though they were not within

His target market. But they weren't His priority. Jesus knew His primary audience, a very narrow band of people.

Develop the Essence of Your Central Message

President Franklin D. Roosevelt was once asked how long it would take to prepare an address on a particular theme. "That depends on how long you want me to speak," the president answered. "If you want an hour on the issue, I can be ready in two days. If you want thirty minutes, it will take me a week. If you want five minutes, it may take a month to prepare." FDR knew that arriving at the essence is one of the most demanding of all exercises.

Great people in history are often remembered because of their ability to express their life message, and to do it often. Winston Churchill was announced as the speaker for a public meeting during the dark days of World War II. The full text of his address was: "Never give up. Never give up! Never, never, never give up!"

....

> Great people in history are often remembered because of their ability to express their life message, and to do it often.

....

Abraham Lincoln is memorialized not for the hundreds of orations he delivered over a public life that spanned three decades, but for a thoughtful speech of less than 200 words. It's called The Gettysburg Address.

Jesus demonstrated His focus in a concise message, which one of the gospel writers recorded like this: "The time has come. . . . The kingdom of God is near. Repent and believe the good news!" (Mark 1:15).

First, Jesus established the immediate importance of His message. Second, He delivered the heart of His message—"The kingdom of God is before you, embodied in Me." And third, He gave a solid close—"Here's what you need to do."

Have you noticed that successful candidates for political office are often those who are able to communicate one point clearly? Challenger Ronald Reagan scored a TKO over incumbent Jimmy Carter in the 1980 presidential debates by asking one simple question: "Are you better off now than you were four years ago?" In 2008, Barak Obama shortened his appeal to the voters to two marketable promises: "Hope and Change." Those two words won him the White House.

We've all had to endure people who take hours of our time, filling the air with 200 words a minute, with gusts up to 550. When they're finished, we can't remember anything they said.

What would your friends say is your message? Do they say, "Beats me, but he's a nice guy"? Well, my dog's nice, too, but I wouldn't ask her how to live more effectively. We need to think about the message we want to leave behind. What is it that you believe in and want to communicate so badly that you are willing to reduce it to an understandable core?

Realize the Experience of a Limited Time Frame

Everyone works within a limited time frame. You are playing out the finite number of days assigned to you, and it may be this very ticking of the clock that will encourage you to make something happen.

In 1974, Ara Parseghian brought Notre Dame's Fighting Irish football team from South Bend, Indiana, to the Los Angeles Coliseum for the final game of the regular season. His opponent was the USC Trojans, a national rival for 48 years. Although the Trojans were favored by four points, the Irish had been rated the top defensive team in the nation. The stage was set for a game well worth the price of admission.

The contest began in a familiar pattern as the Irish pulled out in front with some unexpected play-action passes. By halftime, the score stood in Notre Dame's favor, 24-6. It looked like an easy win for the Irish.

Then came 17 minutes of agony for Ara Parseghian and the Fighting Irish. The 84,000 spectators at the Coliseum—and the millions watching by television—saw the Trojan offensive and defensive units explode to life. In those historic 17 minutes, USC scored 49 points, crossing the goal line almost at will.

Tony Davis opened the second half with a remarkable 102-yard touchdown sprint through the entire Irish defense. A few plays later he scored again. Pat Haden took care of whatever Tony Davis left undone. By the time the dust settled in the Southern California twilight, the scoreboard told the electrifying tale: USC, 55; Notre Dame, 24. That incredible comeback became a part of sports history.

A limited time frame will either immobilize a person in fear or energize him in expectancy. For USC, it did the latter. The Trojans' sense of urgency propelled them to extraordinary performance.

Imagine that this morning, as you arrived at your office, your phone tone indicated a newly arrived text. It's from God—letting you know in 140-characters-or-less that you've only got 42 months before your time on earth is finished, and you'll be joining Him beyond. How would you react?

Jesus held a strong sense of the limited time He had to accomplish His mission. He began His public work at age 30. Within the first few months, He drew 12 men to Himself and began to spend concentrated time with them, explaining that He had to go to Jerusalem and suffer many things at the hands of the recognized religious leaders. He even told them that He would be killed and that He would be raised to life again three days later. Just past His thirtieth birthday, He heard the clock ticking. He knew He was running out of time.

On the night before He was killed, Jesus offered a marvelous prayer. He began it by saying that the time had come—that He had finished the work God gave Him to do (see John 17:4). No lament about a job missed; no regret that time ran out before He could complete all of His tasks. Just a simple, matter-of-fact statement that His work was done.

If you knew you had only 42 months left, would you be more focused than you are today? Most of us have a deep-seated sense of immortality. We live our lives as if we had all the time in the world . . . but we don't. Statistically, the odds are high that someone reading this book has no more than three-and-a-half years left. The more we realize our time limits, the more convinced we become of the need to focus.

> The more we realize our time limits,
> the more convinced we become
> of the need to focus.

A few years ago, Jack Nicholson and Morgan Freeman joined forces in *The Bucket List*, a movie that quickly became iconic. The premise: two men meet in a shared hospital room, with medical conditions that signal their coming demise. The rest of the film is devoted to their exploits to live life to the max and experience their every fantasy so that they could declare their lives well lived.

Jesus is far wiser than the characters played by Nicholson and Freeman: with the short time between here and heaven, a life well lived focuses on the divine assignments that characterize a well-lived life. "Well done, good and faithful servant" (Matt. 25:21) was not at the bottom of the Bucket List, but it is the welcome extended by the Savior to all who have followed His lead.

Understand the Significance of Your Personal Responsibility

Most everything I needed to know in life I learned in high school football. My team was a melting pot of ethnic flavors, coached by a similarly blended cohort of committed men. My mentor was a 6' 5" 260-pound persuader named Manuel Peñaflor.

As the giant on the defensive line playing right tackle (I weighed in at 172 pounds, minus gear), Manny would often start with me when demonstrating a point. One day, as we lined up for scrimmage, Coach decided to capture a teaching opportunity. He had a peculiar way of seizing our attention—he would grab your face mask and pull you up real close so you wouldn't miss a single word.

On this particular day, he hooked my facemask and yelled in his distinctive Hispanic English, "Chank, you're one defensive tackle, not the whole team. I don't want you playing the whole football field. Here's your job."

He released his grip on my helmet and then used his foot to scratch a 10-foot by 10-foot square around my spot on the line. "Chank, you see this square?" I couldn't miss it. "This square is yours; that's *your* field. Anybody from the other team who comes into this square, it's your job to put them on their butt. You got that?" I got it.

When he was convinced I understood my assignment, he moved to the middle guard, Ernie Norton, and went through the same theatrics. Property rights were assigned in 100-square-foot increments to five linemen and two linebackers. None of us could ever say we didn't know what was expected of us. We knew our personal responsibilities on that field when the other guys had the ball.

I think of Manny often when I tense up over what needs to be done on a global scale. I have a tendency to become frustrated, then fatalistic, because I can't get my arms around all there is to do. It's at those moments that I need to remember: I'm not assigned the whole planet. I've only been entrusted with a particular slice of it. That is the portion of the world for which God will one day hold me accountable.

Jesus knew His area of personal responsibility. He stated it clearly when He addressed a large crowd: "I have come down from heaven not to do my will but to do the will of him who sent me" (John 6:38). He also said He would welcome everyone whom God would give him.

At this point, there's a great temptation to read this as yet another goal-setting challenge. That is definitely *not* the point. Goals presume that you and I can decide what the future will be. Perhaps you've attended those seminars where you're challenged to "just name what you're going to do, and how much income you're going to create next year. You have the power to speak it into existence." That is a lie. "Name it and claim it" sells books and fills arenas, but it's see-through theology.

An exceptionally wise man of history named Solomon said at the peak of his career: "The dice are thrown; but the LORD determines every outcome" (Prov. 16:33, *GOD'S WORD*.) Was he right? When he was an old man, looking back at life with the voice of experience, he said, "The race is not to the swift or the battle to the strong, nor does food come to the wise or wealth to the brilliant or favor to the learned" (Eccles. 9:11). God says we can't figure out the future.

Jesus did not come to earth for "results." He came to do what God told Him to do. These were the results: "All that the Father gives me will come to me" (John 6:37). The results were in God's hands.

Unfortunately, I meet people every day who are committed to results—their intended results, established by them, for their own benefit—and will do anything to get them. God will never ask you, "What did you achieve?" He'll ask, "Did you serve Me?" He will ask, "Were you faithful?" Jesus said, "Those who come to Me—that's up to God. What happens when they come to Me—that's My responsibility; I will never drive them away."

Many people consider their lives upside down because they don't see results. I often ask, "Are you doing what God wants you to do?" Sometimes they say, "Yes, but it's not working." I tell them, "Yes, it is. It may not accomplish what you expected—God never said it would. He only said it's what He wants you to do."

When Manny drew that 100-square-foot box for me, he said my responsibility was to knock down any enemy player who dared enter. The opposition might score a touchdown around the opposite end, but I couldn't do anything about that. He wouldn't criticize me for it as long as I did my job.

Mastering Your Life

You may be thinking that you should broaden your life rather than narrow your focus. Realize that your effectiveness will increase when you focus. Take a minute to write down your own focus in each of the four areas we've covered:

Specific Audience:

Concise Message:

Finite Time Frame:

Personal Responsibility:

Are you satisfied with what you observe in each area? Is your effectiveness heightened or minimized by your current status? What do you need to do to narrow your focus in the out-of-focus areas?

] 12 [

EXCELLENCE

Early in my Kingdom leadership travels, I came to appreciate one of the genuine statesmen of the Christian business world. His name was Fred Smith Sr., a man whose business experience spanned the middle of the twentieth century. He served on more corporate boards than most people can list and was asked to speak at events for Christian business leaders all over the world. But what attracted me to Fred was his wisdom.

As a young boy, Fred cut his right hand on a broken mason jar. An inept country doctor mistreated the injury, rendering Fred's hand nearly unusable. Fred's perspective on his hand had more power than any healthy fist could equal. "You see this hand? This is all I can do with it," he would tell a spellbound audience. "But let me tell you something. This hand is not my problem. It's a fact of life. Do you know the difference? A problem is something you can do something about. There's nothing I can do about my hand. A fact of life is something you can't change. So you accept that and get on with your life."

Fred was a wonderful role model of the pursuit of excellence. I heard him say, "I get so tired of hearing people tell me about the problems that hold them back from achieving what they want to achieve in life. Truth is, most of them are confused. They've confused their facts of life with problems. They think they can fix something that can't be fixed, and they're stifled by problems that deny them their future."

This is the final element in our LifeMastery package. By performing to your full potential, you will exceed the expectations of those who live to minimize others.

By performing to your full potential,
you will exceed the expectations of those
who live to minimize others.

Many of these folks have a tremendous desire to regularly remind you that you will never be much more than you are today. They aim to keep you from realizing what you could really be. People who are excellent do not necessarily win the accolades of their contemporaries.

What we want to discover is the often-unappreciated potential in each of us. And we'll see that there is one whose approval and acclaim we *can* live for, someone who wants us to become all that we were created to be.

Unfortunately, most of us are driven by the bell curve mentality. We generally are most comfortable within the heart of the bell, where 80 percent of the population resides. When we start moving toward the leading edge of the curve, we make people uncomfortable.

Early in my business life, I was given the opportunity to transfer from an administrative support role in the purchasing department to a newly created position in the sales department. The company specialized in securing six-figure contracts with clients in the home-building industry, but my field of responsibility was to take our product directly to the retail buyer, with sales averaging about 3 percent of the company's normal contract value in its primary market. Simply stated: it took 33 "deals" from my category to equal 1 "deal" from the other departments. I was no threat to my older, wiser cohorts.

That is, I didn't appear to be a threat. Over the next year, my field of pursuit *blossomed*. No one had considered that the profit percentage potential of my sales might exceed that of the large-scale contracts. It turned out that the company made more money on 15 of my sales than it did on 1 of the larger contracts. Within 12 months, the profit contribution from my activities was greater than that of any other sales executive in the firm—some of whom had been in the industry for longer than I had been alive! The department that had been slighted by the veterans was now getting noticed!

How did they react to my unexpected success? If you are guessing they convened celebrations in my honor, think again. Rather than plaques and backslaps, my team began to receive scrutiny and backstabs. This dark-horse addition to the company stable threatened the long-time teammates. Their security was challenged by the presence of a young, lightly trained co-worker who had found a way to produce.

You don't always win friends when you win.

Only the man who excels has to answer the criticisms of those who challenge competence. The perfect example of this is Jesus Christ. Although He was popular, He faced plenty of criticism from religious and political leaders and former followers who expected a different kind of Messiah. But criticism and unpopularity never stopped Jesus from pursuing excellence in all He did. Let's see how His example can be a model for us.

Aspire to Deliver an Exemplary Performance

Jesus visited Capernaum early in His ministry and spoke at the local synagogue on the Sabbath. His teaching amazed the people; He didn't teach like the trained teachers of the law. "He taught as one who had authority" (Matt 7:29).

Religious teachers at that time spent years learning about the law and studying commentaries on it. These guys had a corner on the market. They were organized: "Teachers of the Law, Local 425"—dues-paying members of the religious communicator's club. People had become used to their droning performances, and public expectations were low. Then, here comes an unknown from the little borough of Nazareth. He lands in the middle of this scene and begins to communicate. The people wake up, take notice and realize how different this is from the normal chatter.

The religious leaders didn't take too kindly to this newcomer for several reasons. First, the religious leadership in that society was strictly upper crust; only a certain pedigree allowed you to break into that group. If you wanted to be a priest, your family had to spring from the tribe of Levi, the group entrusted with the priesthood some 15 centuries before. The problem was that Jesus hailed from the tribe of Judah—known in the past for its prominent political leaders, not its spiritual leaders. He didn't fit the accepted criteria for a spiritual authority.

Second, everyone knew that teachers needed to have formal training. The foremost religious educator of Jesus' day was a man named Gamaliel, whose students learned at his feet in the Temple training institute. Among his notable students in the first century was a man named Saul of Tarsus, a Pharisee of some distinction. On the other hand, among those who had never seen the inside of the Temple training institute was Jesus, a carpenter from Nazareth. Claiming no acceptable rabbi as His mentor, Jesus came to the party with no recognized alma mater. He was no easy player to evaluate: you couldn't judge Him from His résumé (He didn't have one). You were forced to evaluate Him on His own merits, something His critics were unprepared to do.

A friend of mine is the CEO of one of the largest firms in his industry. He supervises a staff of nearly 200 people and oversees business activity measured in the hundreds of millions of dollars annually. This guy is a winner at what he does. Not only is his company highly profitable, but he also serves in the senior leadership of the trade association that involves all of his competitive peers.

Recently, he had a breakfast meeting with three prestigious bankers striving to win his company's business. During the course of their table talk they began swapping stories about their experiences in business school. As the bankers compared pedigrees and alma maters, they turned to my friend and asked him where he got his MBA. "I don't have an MBA," he answered.

Naturally, they asked him where he did his undergraduate work. My friend leaned forward as if to share a secret. Then he dropped this bombshell: "I didn't go to college."

Dumb luck arrived about that time. I walked into the restaurant while this conversation was in progress. At the moment the bankers' jaws fell on the table, I saw my friend and came over to greet him. He told me later that if I hadn't interrupted them at that moment, they might still be fumbling for a response.

What was the problem? The bankers couldn't reconcile this man's exemplary accomplishments with his rudimentary résumé. A truck had just run over all their tidy assumptions about the prerequisites for professional achievement.

Wouldn't it be tragic if you decided your future was limited by your past? Some people would tell my friend that his lack of college would keep him from responsible management positions. But his background is not his problem; it's just a fact of life. He accepted it long ago. He demonstrates that our past doesn't need to limit us in pursuing our mission.

> Our past doesn't need to limit us
> in pursuing our mission.

My friend was prepared for life even though he didn't go through all the "right" training programs. I've seen college graduates who aren't prepared, and I've found people who are prepared who never attended college. The question shouldn't be "Where did you go to school?" but rather, "Are you educated?"

Jesus wasn't formally educated in the schools where the Pharisees got their theological degrees. But He was thoroughly prepared.

If you have a dream that doesn't make sense to anyone but you, don't let the doomsayers near it. Protect it. Nurture it. Commit it to the Creator of every dream that honors Him, and give the rest of your life to turning it into reality.

In the process, expect to be criticized. People won't understand what you are doing and will attack you. Count on it.

Anticipate the Criticism of the Ever-Present Detractors

In case it hasn't dawned on you, the world is not standing on the sidelines cheering you to victory. In fact, they're usually on the opposing side of the field, whooping it up when you get tackled for a loss. Sometimes you get the feeling that public opinion runs the direction of universal antagonism—people don't seem to want anyone to win. If someone starts to shine, the goal is to tarnish him as quickly as possible.

You don't serve long in the role of an aspiring world-changer before you run into sniper fire. Jesus sure experienced it. Shortly after His powerful performance in Capernaum, He started getting flak from different pockets of His peer group. Let's look at some of the groups that attacked Him.

Family

This might surprise you. We tend to have this nice traditional picture of Mary and Joseph and their wonderful little family. We can almost see them gathering for the holidays with never a hint of dissension. What a warm, embracing, self-worth affirming group!

Well, not exactly. When Jesus started speaking in public, His family recoiled. In fact, one time He spoke in a house and the crowd grew so great that the disciples couldn't even eat. When His family heard about it, they decided to go and take charge of Him because, they said, "He is out of his mind" (Mark 3:21).

This sounds like the dark side of the Holy Family. Jesus had become a family embarrassment. How could they let Him run loose? What would the neighbors think? How would they explain to their friends at the synagogue? The situation required decisive action.

So they went to get Him. On arrival, they sent a message to the front of the crowd: "your mother and brothers are outside looking for you" And how did Jesus respond? He looked at those around him and said, "Here are my mother and brothers!" (Mark 3:31-34). Jesus made it clear that his family didn't consist of people who shared a DNA chain with Him. Rather, it consisted of those who shared with Him a common ideology.

Jesus' family grew troubled that He was performing at a level beyond their comfort zone. I don't think they were unusual. Family can be our best supporters. But all too often, when we step out and do something different, family doesn't understand. And usually when they don't understand, they try to pull us down to a more comfortable level.

Community

Shortly after this encounter with His family, Jesus did visit His hometown. On the Sabbath, He again went into the synagogue to teach. And again, the people who heard Him were amazed. Then they started analyzing what they had seen and heard. "Where did this man get this wisdom and these miraculous powers? . . . Isn't this the carpenter's son? Isn't his mother's name Mary, and aren't his brothers James, Joseph, Simon and Judas? Aren't all his sisters with us? Where then did this man get all these things? And they took offense at Him (Matt. 13:54-57).

Look how quickly they moved from amazement to offense. What happened in that short time? The crowd began to chatter. And what did they chatter about? They questioned how this man, who was one of them, got his "stuff." They didn't ask if it was valid. They assumed it wasn't because it was unconventional. Jesus didn't go to college. He didn't have the right job. He didn't have the right family background. It just wasn't what they expected. So they assumed He was wrong.

It was then that Jesus uttered those oft-quoted words:

> Only in his hometown and in his own house is a prophet without honor (Matt. 13:57).

Are there exceptions? Yes. But many have felt what He felt that day. There's no harder crowd to win over than the folks who knew you when, and who think they know why your current effectiveness may not last. It's hard for many people to watch a neighbor succeed and wish him well. In fact, it's often the motivation to launch an attack that might pull him or her back down to the mean once again.

Leaders

Jesus encountered resistance from a third area: the religious and political elite. Of all the groups we've looked at, it makes sense that these folks should be the most offended, for Jesus challenged their power base. Still, their methods of attack might surprise us. One time they came up to Jesus and said, "Aren't we right in saying that you are a Samaritan and demon-possessed?" (John 8:48).

Think of the worst ethnic slur possible, and that's what these people used. They called Jesus a half-breed. They said He was worthless and demon-possessed. They used the most outrageous epithets to put Him down.

It was so blatant that Jesus couldn't ignore all of it. He passed over the ethnic slur, but He addressed the question of His spiritual identity: "I am not possessed by a demon . . . but I honor my Father and you dishonor me" (John 8:49). The leaders shot back, "We know that you are demon-possessed! . . . Who do you think you are?" (John 8:52-53.)

Who do you think you are? Only eternity will reveal how many people faded from view, their potential unrealized, because of words like these. We probably can all look back and find wounds inflicted by those who were threatened when we tried to fulfill our potential. Perhaps they feared an out-of-control ego or an unwillingness to be "normal." Maybe they thought us as out of step with reality. If we listened to them, we climbed back into the same miry pit of mediocrity that ensnares most people.

....

We probably can all look back and find wounds inflicted by those who were threatened when we tried to fulfill our potential. If we listened to them, we climbed back into the same miry pit of mediocrity that ensnares most people.

....

Based on the opposition He received from family, community and leadership, it's amazing we ever heard of Jesus. If we listened to the majority voices, we'd have to believe He couldn't go anywhere—that we'd never hear any more from Him. But the opposite happens. From the time of these denunciations until the end of His life, we find that He performed more and more beyond their expectations. Even within His lifetime, vindication came.

Await the Vindication of the Final Appraisal

Some homespun sage put it bluntly: "It ain't over 'til it's over." Excellence isn't a snapshot; it is the epilogue for the mission-driven person who has persevered to the end.

A great figure of history illustrates this truth well. His mother died at an early age. His formal education was minimal. At 22, his first business failed. Like many who fail in business, he decided to run for political office. At age 23, he lost the race for a local office. At age 24, he started another business and failed again. Fortunately, the next year he was elected to the state legislature. During his term, his fiancée died.

At age 27, he suffered a nervous breakdown. At 29, he ran for Speaker of the House and was defeated. At 31, he ran for a state elector and lost. At 34, he ran for Congress and lost. But he didn't quit. He ran again two years later, and at age 37, he was elected. Two years later, however, he was defeated in a bid for reelection.

Talk about a midlife crisis! By age 40, this man had experienced two business failures, the death of a loved one, a nervous breakdown and several political election defeats. And it got worse. At age 46, he ran for Senate and lost. A year later, he was listed on the party ticket as candidate for vice president. The ticket lost. At 49, he lost another race for Senate.

Time to place your bets on his life. What do you think? Is he a winner or a loser? Should he fade from view and accept his mediocrity? Is he just a dreamer with delusions of grandeur? What would you counsel him to do with his life?

Some time ago, I was riding in the top deck of a double-decker bus in London, taking in a one-day tour of the city before my flight from Heathrow Airport. As we rounded a corner in downtown London, our guide pulled alongside a bronze statue standing in the middle of a traffic circle. Guess who it was? The very man who had made it a habit to lose in his pursuit of a life mission: Abraham Lincoln.

I'm glad Lincoln didn't give up his dream. At the age of 51, he was elected President of the United States, and he led this country during its most crucial test. Had he folded his tent and gone home rather than press on, the future of the world might well have been altered. Instead, throughout the world he is regarded as one of our greatest statesmen.

Jesus was vindicated even during His lifetime. Look at His final appraisal, first from His competitors—the men who vied for the affection and attention of the community. They sent a delegation to Him. Though they were trying to trap Him, they recognized who He was: "Teacher, we know you are a man of integrity. You aren't swayed by men, because you pay no attention to who they are; but you teach the way of God in accordance with the truth" (Mark 12:14). His enemies still didn't like him, but they had to admit the obvious: "You've gone far beyond what we ever thought you could do." I don't think these men ever spoke any harder words.

It's interesting to see what happened to the man who stood in judgment over Jesus: Pilate. His role in the execution of Jesus was curious. He admitted to the religious leaders, "You brought me this man as one who was inciting the people to rebellion. I have examined him in your presence and have found no basis for your charges against him" (Luke 23:14). Pilate then sent Jesus to Herod, the titular king of the Jewish people, and not even Herod could find anything against Jesus.

This was like unleashing the Washington press corps on one guy and saying, "Call every deep throat informant you know and tell him to spill his guts on Jesus." They followed Him, they photographed Him, they quizzed people and still they couldn't find anything amiss. The execution of Jesus was purely a political act; there was no basis for it in fact.

Jesus' followers also vindicated Him. You would think if there was any dirt on Jesus, it would be known to those closest to Him. Certainly the "kiss and tell" phenomenon is not new. But the man closest to Him, John, had nothing to say against Him, and neither did any of His other followers. In fact, they concluded He was God!

I am overwhelmed by the example of Jesus Christ. In His life, He established a stimulating example that can influence the way you and I live today. He showed it in the way He pursued excellence. He showed us that excellence is not an objective standard set by some human committee. Excellence goes beyond what people are prepared to see in your life. Whatever limitation the world wants to impose, it can be overcome when we pursue a God-ordained mission.

Mastering Your Life

People want to be able to explain away excellence by pointing to education or upbringing or circumstances as the reason for personal achievement. Excellence hinges on escaping the limiting expectations of those around you.

Evaluate on a 10-point scale what kind of performance most people expect from you because of your résumé:

1   2   3   4   5   6   7   8   9   10

On the same scale, how would you currently rate your overall performance in life?

1   2   3   4   5   6   7   8   9   10

Also on a 10-point scale, what do you know your potential to be when considering the magnifying factor of God in your life?

1   2   3   4   5   6   7   8   9   10

Finally, what is one thing you can do now to move the number on the second scale closer to the number on the third scale?

_____

_____

_____

_____

_____

_____

At this moment, you may be one decision short of a significant breakthrough in your life. You may be reviewing a checkered past, wondering if it isn't masochistic to keep chasing your vision. Your head is pounding a cadence that your heart finds increasingly difficult to step to. How long do you have to wait to be rewarded?

For me, it helps to remember a dank dungeon cell and a prisoner awaiting execution. This man had time to write one last letter to a young friend a continent away. Some would say this prisoner had been a fool: a man whose prominence and promise were scrapped decades earlier in favor of an unpopular cause. He had given his prime years to recruit men and women to a radical message of transformation made possible by an obscure Hebrew carpenter. The writer, whom we know as Paul the Apostle, gave his young protégé Timothy the encouragement you may need today to "go for it":

> The time has come for me to leave this life. I have fought the good fight, I have finished the race, I have kept the faith. Now a crown is being held for me—a crown for being right with God. The Lord, the judge who judges rightly, will give the crown to me on that day—not only to me but to all those who have waited with love for him to come again (2 Tim. 4:6-8, *NCV*).

Epilogue

This book has been woven together from two very different life stories. One is the story of my life; the other is the story of Jesus' life.

My textbook "Type A" lifestyle was radically reoriented more than 30 years ago by a life-purpose statement. Since that time, I have used that synopsis as a compass to direct the course my life. During that time, I have discovered two amazing things.

The first is that Cheri and I have made some radical shifts in our lives. In 1981, I left the prospect of a secure executive position with a multinational corporation to start my own business. Though most entrepreneurial ventures are motivated by the founder's desire to advance professionally or financially, my business was launched to allow me to maintain freedom and flexibility to pursue my purpose statement. It was the best means for us to advance our mission.

In 1984, I sold my start-up business and founded Priority Living, a nonprofit organization designed to serve business and professional men and women. It was the structure through which I would increase the leverage to advance my purpose.

I enjoy the greatest of all setups: I am the CEO of an organization whose purpose mirrors my own!

When asked how we managed to make two potentially stress-laden decisions of this magnitude within five years, I point to our purpose statement. Choosing the course that best advanced our mission made these decisions clear.

After moving through seasons of a career cycle that often result in midlife crisis, I have seen the value of a stable benchmark against which to measure our activities and commitments. As a couple, Cheri and I have spent more than 40 years together, and our purpose has been a North Star, allowing us to constantly refine our direction and recalibrate our activities. Through very challenging seasons and situations, we've always had the confidence that we had a long-term view that made sense of the short-term demands and distractions.

My second discovery was that we represent a tiny minority. Most men and women have never thought through the question of their purpose in life.

It is possible that you may be one of those who has never put into print your vision for life. If we have the occasion to meet in the future, it would be my hope to hear that you accepted the challenge to think this subject through to a conclusion. Living on purpose is the only way to go!

Much of this book has been about my experiences. To be honest, you can take my experiences or leave them, but the same is not true of the life of Jesus Christ. His remarkable blueprint for living can forever transform your sense of potential . . . if you let it.

If you have never seriously considered the value of a personal relationship with Jesus Christ, now may be your moment of truth. Far beyond His role as a model for life, Jesus came to offer Himself as your substitute.

Let me explain. In God's economy, everything has a price. Every decision we make carries the certainty of future consequence. Each time you make a decision to deny your conscience and God's perfect standards—in what you say, think or do—you accumulate indebtedness before God. He doesn't just turn His back on that debt; someday, you will have to pay up.

God calls these actions that fall short of His perfect standard "sin," and those sins have a price: separation from Him for eternity. That fact would have guaranteed you a hopeless future had it not been for Jesus Christ. When He came to earth, He came to solve your problem with God. He came to take upon Himself the penalty for your sins and the sins of all humanity. He came to settle the score with God the Father for you.

God unleashed all of the just penalty for your sins on Jesus as He hung on a cross. During those agonizing hours of His death, He suffered the full effects of God's justice to make your pardon possible. When He died, the entire settlement for your failure before God was taken care of, once and for all. He paid a debt He didn't owe in order to make you free.

Death. It was your fate. But it became Jesus' choice instead. Three days after His death, He came to life and left the tomb in which He had been buried. He said He had the power to take up His life again, and He did. He said He had the power to forgive your sin and to give you eternal life, and He does. He says He will vouch for you before His Father at the final judgment and will see to it that you join Him for eternity.

But there's something you must do to receive these benefits and enter into a vibrant, living relationship with God. The Bible describes it as accepting Jesus: believing that He is who He claimed to be, that He did what He said He would do and that He is the only one who can save you from God's judgment.

If you've never made the conscious decision to surrender your life to Jesus Christ, the smartest move is to do it now. You may express these thoughts to Him in a simple prayer:

> *God, I know I have done things in my life that aren't acceptable to You. I admit those things and ask You to forgive me. I believe that Jesus died to pay the debt for my sins. I believe that He is Your son and that He rose from death and returned to You in heaven. I want to surrender my life to Him now and receive the gift of eternal life. I open my life to Your presence. Thank You for loving me enough to die for me on the cross.*

If you have expressed this desire to God, you've joined countless millions before you who have entrusted their lives to God's care. You have received a part in God's great purpose for the men and women in His family—a purpose articulated by Jesus just before He returned to heaven:

> All authority in heaven and on earth is given to me. Therefore go and make disciples of all nations, baptizing them in the name of the Father and of the Son and of the Holy Spirit, and teaching them to obey everything I have commanded you. And surely

I am with you always, to the very end of the age (Matt. 28:18-20).

Those are the marching orders issued by Jesus the King to the men and women who have come to believe in and follow Him. Your purpose—your life mission—is a piece in the larger mosaic of His redemptive purpose to bring a wandering race back into relationship with our loving Creator. Join us in that mission. And start now!

THE MASTER'S PROGRAM

In 1997, Bob Shank wove the principles of LifeMastery together with additional Kingdom leadership strategies and created a three-year leadership-mentoring program. Designed for men and women who have spent great time and money refining their careers—without an opportunity to give similar attention to their calling—they knew what they were *paid for* but did not yet know what they were *made for*. The leap *from Marketplace success* to *Kingdom significance* was the unique value proposition offered in The Master's Program.

Since then, thousands of Christian leaders—from marketplace and ministry backgrounds—have participated in and benefited from The Master's Program. Now established in dozens of key regional sites in North America, The Master's Program coaches serious Christians to find the *balance* that authenticates their Kingdom leadership, the *margin* that makes them available for Kingdom engagement and the *focus* to help them distinguish between good works and the work for which God made them. The Master's Program may be the next key step in your journey to LifeMastery.

For information about participation
in The Master's Program, visit our website:

WWW.MASTERSPROGRAM.ORG

To contact Bob Shank regarding his availability for speaking on these themes, contact him through:

The Master's Program
4500 Campus Drive, Suite 550
Newport Beach, CA 92660
Phone: (949) 756-2096